THE COMPLETE

KETO DIET

COOKBOOK FOR BEGINNERS |

100 Healthy, Delicious,
and Nutritious High-Protein, Low-Carb Recipes
with 28 - Day Meal Plan for Easy Weight Loss
| Includes Full-Color Pictures |

Mia Norman

Disclaimer
The information provided in this cookbook is for general informational purposes only. All recipes and nutritional information are offered in good faith and are believed to be accurate at the time of publication. However, the author makes no representation or warranty of any kind, express or implied, regarding the accuracy, adequacy, validity, reliability, availability, or completeness of any information contained in this cookbook.

The recipes in this cookbook are intended for educational and entertainment purposes. Always consult with a qualified healthcare professional or nutritionist before starting any new diet or exercise program, especially if you have pre-existing medical conditions, are pregnant, nursing, or are taking medication. The author and publisher disclaim any liability for any adverse effects or consequences resulting from using the recipes or suggestions herein.

Individual results may vary. The nutritional information provided is estimated and can vary depending on the ingredients and brands used. Readers are encouraged to seek professional advice regarding specific health or dietary concerns.
By using this cookbook, you accept this disclaimer in full.

Table of Contents:

Table of Contents:

INTRODUCTION

Welcome to the exciting world of the ketogenic diet, a revolutionary approach to nutrition that has helped millions achieve their health and weight loss goals. The keto diet isn't just about shedding pounds—it's about adopting a healthier lifestyle that benefits your mind, body, and soul. This guide is designed to take you by the hand and lead you through the basics of keto, helping you understand why it works and how it can be adapted to fit your needs.

What is Keto?

The ketogenic, or keto, diet is a low-carbohydrate, high-fat eating plan that drives the body into ketosis, a state of metabolic efficiency where the body burns fat for fuel instead of glucose. This shift comes from drastically reducing carbohydrate intake and replacing it with fat, which causes your body to use fat as its primary energy source. Ketosis is characterized by the production of ketones, compounds that serve as an alternate energy source for the brain and body.

The origins of the keto diet trace back to the 1920s, initially developed to help control seizures in patients with epilepsy. However, it has gained immense popularity recently for its effectiveness in weight loss, energy stabilization, and potential benefits in various neurological illnesses, diabetes, and even cancer.

CHAPTER 1: Keto Basics

1. Understanding Macronutrients

Macronutrients are the cornerstone of any diet. They include carbohydrates, proteins, and fats, each playing a critical role in body functions and overall health. Understanding how these macronutrients work and their caloric contributions—carbohydrates and proteins provide about four calories per gram, while fats provide 9—helps manage dietary needs and reach health goals.

- **Fats:** Approximately 70-80% of daily calories come from fats. These include healthy fats like avocados, nuts, seeds, olive oil, and fatty fish, essential for maintaining energy levels and supporting bodily functions.
- **Proteins:** Around 25-30% of calories are derived from proteins, which include meats, poultry, eggs, and dairy products. Adequate protein intake helps maintain muscle mass while ensuring that excess protein does not disrupt the state of ketosis.
- **Carbohydrates:** Carbohydrate intake is restricted to about 5-10% of daily calories, often below 50 grams per day. This limited intake of carbs forces the body to switch from glucose metabolism to fat metabolism, producing ketones that serve as an alternative energy source

2. Explaining Macronutrients and Their Role in the Keto Diet

The distribution and type of macronutrients consumed in a ketogenic diet are pivotal to success. The goal is to adjust the typical macronutrient distribution to a high-fat, moderate-protein, and low-carbohydrate ratio to encourage the body to enter and maintain ketosis.

- **High-Fat**: Consuming high levels of healthy fats encourages the body to rely on lipids rather than glucose for energy, leading to fat loss and increased energy levels. Sources include avocados, cheese, nuts, and fatty fish like salmon.
- **Moderate-Protein**: Protein intake must be moderated because excessive protein can be converted into glucose, potentially kicking you out of ketosis. Finding the balance is about preserving muscle mass while effectively managing ketosis.
- **Low-Carbohydrate**: Limiting carbs is essential as it lowers the blood glucose levels and insulin spikes, pushing the body to find an alternative energy source—fat, broken down into ketones.

3. Benefits of the Keto Diet

The ketogenic diet offers several compelling health benefits, which have contributed to its popularity:

- **Weight Loss:** Using fat as the primary energy source makes the body more efficient at burning body fat, which can lead to significant weight loss.
- **Improved Blood Sugar Control:** Keto naturally reduces blood sugar levels due to the type of foods you eat. Studies also suggest a ketogenic diet can be a more effective way to manage and prevent diabetes compared to low-calorie diets.
- **Enhanced Brain Function:** Ketones provide an immediate fuel source for the brain. Many people on keto experience sharper cognition, better memory, and improved focus.
- **Increased Energy & Improved Physical Endurance:** You can feel more energized during the day by giving your body a better and more reliable energy source.
- **Appetite Control:** Fat is naturally more satisfying and keeps you in a satiated state longer, which helps control appetite and reduce calorie intake.
- **Support for Heart Health:** When done correctly, the keto diet can reduce cholesterol levels and improve heart health, though attention must be paid.

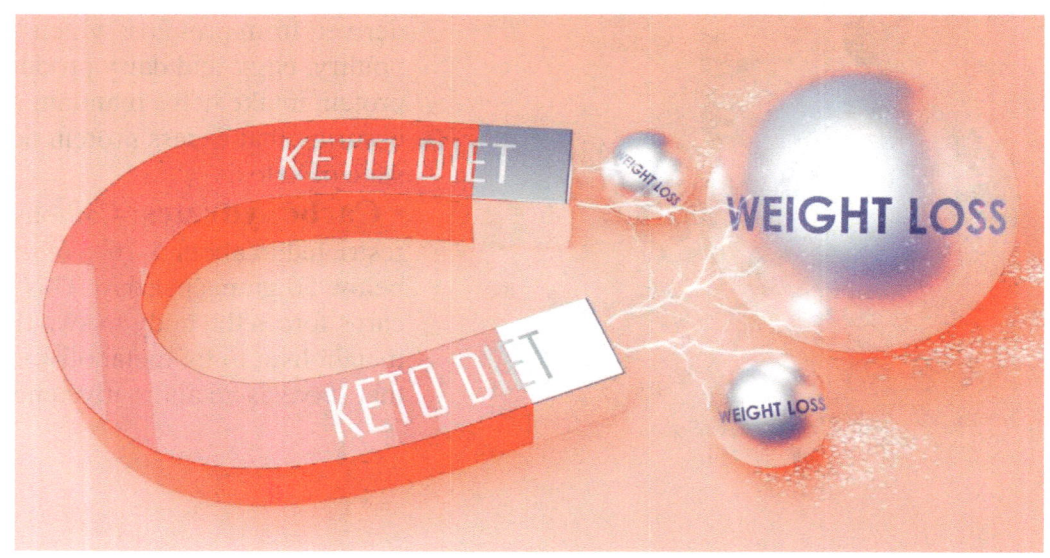

4. Keto Flu: Symptoms and Treatment

As you embark on your ketogenic journey, an initial hurdle you may encounter is the "keto flu," a common experience for newcomers adjusting to low carbohydrate intake. Understanding the symptoms and effective treatments can help you navigate this transitional phase more efficiently and comfortably.

What is Keto Flu?

Keto flu isn't an actual flu but a colloquial term for a collection of symptoms that resemble the flu. These symptoms occur as your body adapts to a new metabolic state called ketosis, which burns fat for fuel instead of carbohydrates.

Symptoms Keto Flu

The onset of keto flu typically occurs within the first few days to a week after reducing carbohydrate intake. Symptoms can vary widely among individuals but commonly include:

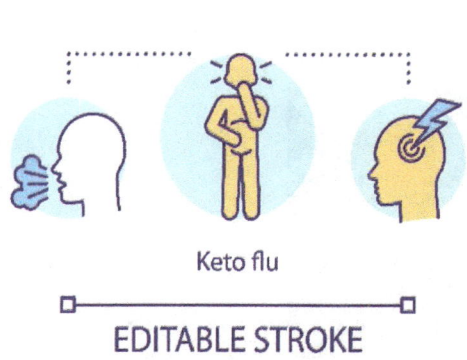

Keto flu

EDITABLE STROKE

Fatigue: As your body switches energy sources, you might feel unusually tired or lethargic.

Headaches: Reduced carbohydrate intake can lead to dehydration and electrolyte imbalances, often resulting in headaches.

Irritability: Many experience mood swings and irritability, a direct result of sugar and caffeine withdrawals.

Dizziness and Light-headedness: These are often due to electrolyte imbalances and changes in blood sugar levels.

Difficulty Sleeping: Diet and energy metabolism changes can temporarily disrupt sleep patterns.

Nausea and Digestive Discomfort: Your digestive system might need time to adapt to a high-fat diet, resulting in nausea or stomach discomfort.

Muscle Cramps and Soreness: Electrolyte imbalances can also cause muscle cramps and aches.

Treatment and Management of Keto Flu

Understanding how to mitigate these symptoms can make the transition to ketosis smoother and more manageable:

• **Stay Hydrated:** Increasing water intake is crucial as high ketone levels can lead to dehydration.

• **Replenish Electrolytes:** Sodium, potassium, and magnesium are essential during the keto transition. Consider adding a pinch of salt to your water, eating foods like avocados and nuts, or taking an electrolyte supplement.

• **Eat More Fats:** Ensure your diet is rich in healthy fats to give your body adequate energy.

• **Balance Your Meals:** Ensure your meals are well-balanced with adequate protein to help keep you satiated.

• **Get Adequate Sleep:** Prioritize good sleep hygiene to help mitigate fatigue and irritability.

• **Gentle Exercise:** While intense workouts might be challenging when experiencing keto flu, gentle activities like walking or yoga can help boost your energy and mood.

• **Patience:** Most importantly, give your body time to adapt. The symptoms of keto flu are temporary, and most people feel better within a week.

5. Foods to Eat and Foods to Avoid

Adopting a ketogenic diet involves more than just reducing your carbohydrate intake; it's about making mindful choices about what you eat every day. Understanding which foods to embrace and which to avoid can make your transition to keto smoother and more effective.

Foods to Eat on Keto

The focus of the ketogenic diet is on high-fat, moderate-protein, and low-carbohydrate foods:

- **Healthy Fats:** Avocado, coconut oil, olive oil, butter, and ghee are excellent for cooking and adding to meals.
- **Proteins:** Choose fatty cuts of meat like steak, ground beef, and pork. Fatty fish such as salmon, mackerel, and sardines are also ideal.
- **Low-Carb Vegetables:** Leafy greens like spinach and kale, and above-ground vegetables such as broccoli, cauliflower, and zucchini.
- **Full-Fat Dairy:** Cheese, cream, and full-fat yogurt can be consumed in moderation.
- **Nuts and Seeds:** Almonds, walnuts, flaxseeds, and chia seeds are great for snacks or as additions to meals.
- **Eggs:** A keto staple, high in protein and fats, and very versatile.

Foods to Avoid on Keto

To maintain ketosis, it's crucial to limit foods high in carbohydrates:
- **Sugary Foods:** Soda, fruit juice, smoothies, cake, ice cream, and candy.
- **Grains and Starches:** Wheat-based products, rice, pasta, and cereals.
- **High-Carb Fruits:** Apples, bananas, oranges, and most other fruits should be avoided except for small portions of berries.
- **Beans and Legumes:** Peas, kidney beans, lentils, chickpeas.
- **Root Vegetables:** Potatoes, sweet potatoes, carrots.
- Some condiments and sauces contain sugar and unhealthy fat.
- **Alcohol:** Many alcoholic drinks can throw you out of ketosis due to their carb content.

CHAPTER 2: Going Keto in Six Steps

Embarking on the ketogenic diet can feel like a daunting task, but breaking it down into manageable steps can make the transition smoother and more successful. Here's a beginner's guide to going keto, tailored to help you understand and efficiently implement the diet into your daily life.

Step 1: Educate Yourself

Before diving into the ketogenic lifestyle, it's crucial to understand what keto is and how it affects your body. The ketogenic diet is a high-fat, moderate-protein, and very low-carbohydrate diet that helps your body switch from using glucose as its primary fuel source to using fat. This metabolic state is known as ketosis. Reading books, reputable online articles and studies can help you understand the benefits and potential challenges of the diet. Learning about the biological processes behind ketosis will equip you with the knowledge to make informed decisions and adjustments to your diet.

Step 2: Clean Out Your Pantry

To commit to a keto lifestyle, start with your environment. Remove high-carb temptations that can derail your efforts. This means getting rid of sugars, grains (like bread, pasta, and rice), starchy vegetables (like potatoes and corn), and fruit (except small portions of berries). Stock your pantry with keto-friendly alternatives such as nuts, seeds, low-carb flour (almond and coconut flour), and sweeteners like stevia or erythritol.

Step 3: Plan Your Meals

Meal planning on the ketogenic diet is essential to avoid the temptation of non-compliant foods. Start by planning out your meals for the week, including snacks. Utilize online resources or keto cookbooks to find recipes that suit your taste and nutritional needs. This can help you maintain the right balance of fats, proteins, and carbs. A plan will reduce grocery shopping stress and minimize food waste, making your diet change efficient and cost-effective.

Step 4: Go Grocery Shopping

With your meal plan, create a grocery list focusing on keto-friendly foods. Your shopping list should include fatty cuts of meat, leafy greens, above-ground vegetables (like broccoli and cauliflower), full-fat dairy products, and healthy fats (like avocados, olive oil, and butter). Stick to your list to avoid impulse buys that aren't keto-friendly. Shopping around the grocery store's perimeter can help you focus on fresh foods and avoid processed items typically found in the center aisles.

Step 5: Start Simple

When beginning a keto diet, simplicity is vital. Start with simple meals that don't require elaborate recipes or unfamiliar ingredients. Essential dishes like grilled meats with a side of sautéed vegetables or salads dressed with high-fat dressings are good starting points. As you become more comfortable with your dietary choices, you can start experimenting with more complex recipes.

Step 6: Monitor Your Progress

Keeping track of your progress is essential for motivation and adjustment. Monitor your weight and other health markers like energy levels, mental clarity, and overall well-being. Tools like food diaries, ketone meters, and fitness trackers can help you understand how your body adapts to the diet. Adjustments may be necessary as your body transitions; observing patterns can guide these changes.

How to Stay on Track

Staying committed to the ketogenic diet requires focus and strategies to maintain your new way of eating:

Set Clear Goals: Define what you hope to achieve with keto, whether it's weight loss, improved energy, or better health overall. Goals keep you motivated.

Use a Tracking App: Apps can help you monitor your daily intake of carbs, proteins, and fats, ensuring you stay within your ketogenic ratios.

Prepare for Challenges: Whether it's a holiday, a social event, or travel, plan how you will navigate these while sticking to your keto diet.

Seek Support: Join keto communities online or find friends who eat keto. Sharing experiences and tips can be incredibly motivating.

Common Problems and How to Overcome Them

✓ **Keto Flu:** This is common in the early stages as your body adapts. Stay hydrated, increase your salt intake, and ensure you're getting enough fat and calories to help mitigate symptoms.

✓ **Plateaus:** Weight loss plateaus happen. To overcome them, reassess your calorie intake, ensure you're getting enough protein, and consider intermittent fasting to boost ketosis.

✓ **Nutrient Deficiencies:** To avoid deficiencies, ensure your diet is varied and includes nutrient-dense foods. Supplements like magnesium, potassium, and vitamin D might be necessary.

✓ **Social Settings:** Eating out or at a friend's house can challenge your diet. Look up the menu beforehand, and don't be shy about asking for dishes that fit your dietary needs.

✓ **Cravings:** These can be tough, especially early on. Find low-carb alternatives, such as keto desserts or snacks, that satisfy your cravings.

By anticipating these common issues and preparing solutions in advance, you can ensure a smoother and more enjoyable keto journey. Each challenge you overcome will strengthen your commitment and bring you closer to your health and wellness goals.

CHAPTER 3: Keto Meal Planning

- **Keep It Simple:** Start with simple recipes that don't require rare ingredients or complex steps. Invest in Quality Containers: Good storage containers are crucial for organizing prepped ingredients and meals.
- **Monitor Your Progress:** Adjust your meal plan based on your dietary results and preferences.
- **Stay Inspired:** Continuously look for new recipes and tweak old favorites to keep your diet exciting and engaging.

28 Day Meal Plan / Week 1

Monday			
Breakfast p.18	**Lunch p.30**	**Dinner p.36**	**Snacks p.72**
Spinach Egg Cheese Muffins / (2 muffins) 240 kcal	Keto Chicken Zoodle Soup / (1 serving) 350 kcal	Bacon-Wrapped Chicken Thighs /(1 serving) 430 kcal	Keto Cheesecake Fat Bombs / (2 fat bombs) 280 kcal
Total Calories: 1300 kcal | Protein: 70g | Fat: 108g | Carbs: 12g			

Tuesday			
Breakfast p.18	**Lunch p.19**	**Dinner p.43**	**Snacks p.76**
Avocado Egg Boats / (1 serving) 320 kcal	Creamy Sausage Egg Casserole / (1 serving) 380 kcal	Keto Pork Carnitas with Avocado Salsa / (1 serving) 370 kcal	Butter Pecan Fat Bombs / (1 serving) 140 kcal
Total Calories: 1210 kcal | Protein: 68g | Fat: 98g | Carbs: 10g			

Wednesday			
Breakfast p.19	**Lunch p.30**	**Dinner p.40**	**Snacks p.73**
Mushroom and Cheddar Omelet / (1 serving) 340 kcal	Low-Carb Broccoli Cheddar Soup / (1 serving) 370 kcal	Keto BBQ Grilled Chicken / (1 serving) 390 kcal	Keto Lemon Bars / (1 serving) 260 kcal
Total Calories: 1360 kcal | Protein: 64g | Fat: 116g | Carbs: 17g			

Thursday			
Breakfast p.25	**Lunch p.31**	**Dinner p.37**	**Snacks p.72**
Fluffy Keto Coconut Pancakes / (1 serving) 270 kcal	Shrimp and Avocado Keto Caesar Salad / (1 serving) 380 kcal	Keto Chicken Alfredo with Zoodles / (1 serving) 420 kcal	Keto Peanut Butter Chocolate Cups / (1 serving) 260 kcal
Total Calories: 1330 kcal | Protein: 74g | Fat: 106g | Carbs: 23g			

Friday			
Breakfast p.26	**Lunch p.33**	**Dinner p.34**	**Snacks p.74**
Keto Sausage and Cheese Breakfast Biscuits / (2 biscuits) 400 kcal	Keto Taco Salad / (1 serving) 420 kcal	Crispy Chicken & Spinach Keto Salad / (1 serving) 350 kcal	Keto Coconut Macaroons / (1 serving) 190 kcal
Total Calories: 1360 kcal | Protein: 70g | Fat: 114g | Carbs: 22g			

Saturday			
Breakfast p.25	**Lunch p.33**	**Dinner p.39**	**Snacks p.72**
Keto "Oatmeal" with Cinnamon and Walnuts / (1 serving) 290 kcal	Tomato Basil Keto Soup / (1 serving) 280 kcal	Keto Chicken Parmesan with Almond Flour / (1 serving) 450 kcal	Keto Cheesecake Fat Bombs / (1 serving) 140 kcal
Total Calories: 1160 kcal | Protein: 55g | Fat: 91g | Carbs: 21g			

Sunday			
Breakfast p.26	**Lunch p.32**	**Dinner p.43**	**Snacks p.73**
Almond Flour Waffles with Butter and Berries / (1 serving) 300 kcal	Keto Creamy Bacon and Spinach Salad / (1 serving) 320 kcal	Keto Balsamic Glazed Pork Loin / (1 serving) 360 kcal	Keto Lemon Bars / (1 serving) 260 kcal
Total Calories: 1240 kcal | Protein: 59g | Fat: 100g | Carbs: 20g			

28 Day Meal Plan / Week 2

Monday

Breakfast p.24	Lunch p.31	Dinner p.36	Snacks p.73
Keto Vanilla Chia Pudding / (1 serving) 130 kcal	Shrimp and Avocado Keto Caesar Salad / (1 serving) 380 kcal	Bacon-Wrapped Chicken Thighs / (1 serving) 430 kcal	Keto Lemon Bars / (1 serving) 260 kcal
Total Calories: 1200 kcal | Protein: 56g | Fat: 99g | Carbs: 17g			

Tuesday

Breakfast p.25	Lunch p.33	Dinnerp.43	Snacks p.76
Fluffy Keto Coconut Pancakes / (2 servings) 270 kcal	Tomato Basil Keto Soup / (1 serving) 280 kcal	Keto Pork Carnitas with Avocado Salsa / (1 serving) 370 kcal	Butter Pecan Fat Bombs / (2 bombs) 280 kcal
Total Calories: 1470 kcal | Protein: 63g | Fat: 124g | Carbs: 27g			

Wednesday

Breakfast p.26	Lunch p.42	Dinner p.32	Snacks p.72
Almond Flour Waffles with Butter and Berries / (2 servings) 600 kcal	Keto Sausage and Cabbage Skillet / (1 serving) 370 kcal	Spicy Thai Chicken Coconut Soup / (1 serving) 350 kcal	Keto Peanut Butter Chocolate Cups / (1 serving) 260 kcal
Total Calories: 1580 kcal | Protein: 67g | Fat: 131g | Carbs: 30g			

Thursday

Breakfast p.25	Lunch p.33	Dinner p.39	Snacks p.74
Keto "Oatmeal" with Cinnamon and Walnuts / (1 serving) 290 kcal	Keto Creamy Taco Salad / (1 serving) 420 kcal	Keto Chicken Parmesan with Almond Flour / (1 serving) 450 kcal	Keto Coconut Macaroons / (1 serving) 190 kcal
Total Calories: 1350 kcal | Protein: 79g | Fat: 105g | Carbs: 23g			

Friday

Breakfast p.26	Lunch p.32	Dinner p.48	Snacks p.73
Keto Sausage and Cheese Breakfast Biscuits /(2 biscuits) 400 k	Creamy Spinach and Bacon Salad (1 serving) 320 kcal	Keto Beef Stroganoff with Zoodles / (1 serving) 370 kcal	Keto Lemon Bars / (1 serving) 260 kcal
Total Calories: 1350 kcal | Protein: 65g | Fat: 118g | Carbs: 22g			

Saturday

Breakfast p.28	Lunch p.30	Dinner p.43	Snacks p.74
Nut Butter & Berry Breakfast Parfait / (1 serving) 220 kcal	Low-Carb Broccoli Cheddar Soup / (1 serving) 370 kcal	Keto Balsamic Glazed Pork Loin / (1 serving) 360 kcal	Keto Coconut Macaroons / (1 serving) 190 kcal
Total Calories: 1140 kcal | Protein: 61g | Fat: 90g | Carbs: 21g			

Sunday

Breakfast p.27	Lunch p.22	Dinner p.43	Snacks p.74
Smoked Salmon and Avocado Breakfast Salad / (1 serving) 380 kcal	Egg-Stuffed Keto Breakfast Peppers / (1 serving) 280 kcal	Keto Pork Carnitas with Avocado Salsa / (1 serving) 370 kcal	Keto Coconut Macaroons / (1 serving) 190 kcal
Total Calories: 1220 kcal | Protein: 73g | Fat: 96g | Carbs: 19g			

Chopping List / Week 1 & Week 2

Week 1

Proteins:

- Chicken thighs – 1.5kg
- Ground sausage – 500g
- Pork shoulder – 1kg
- Shrimp – 400g
- Eggs – 18 large
- Bacon – 12 slices
- Ground beef – 500g

Dairy:

- Heavy cream – 1l
- Shredded cheddar cheese – 300g
- Cream cheese – 100g
- Parmesan cheese – 200g
- Mozzarella cheese – 200g

Vegetables:

- Avocados – 5 large
- Spinach – 500g
- Zucchini – 6 medium
- Bell peppers – 4 medium
- Broccoli – 300g
- Mushrooms – 200g
- Tomatoes (unsweetened, canned) – 4 cups
- Romaine lettuce – 300g

Other Ingredients:

- Pecans, chopped – 30 g
- Almond flour – 500g
- Coconut flour – 200g
- Butter – 300g
- Coconut milk – 2 cans (400ml each)
- Olive oil – 500ml
- Berries (frozen) – 200g
- Erythritol sweetener – 200g
- Vanilla extract – 50ml

Week 2

Proteins:

- Chicken thighs – 1.6kg
- Ground beef – 500g
- Pork shoulder – 1kg
- Smoked salmon – 200g
- Shrimp – 200g
- Eggs – 18 large

Dairy:

- Shredded cheddar cheese – 300g
- Heavy cream – 1L
- Parmesan cheese – 300g

Vegetables:

- Avocados – 5 large
- Spinach – 500g
- Romaine lettuce – 300g
- Zucchini – 6 medium
- Bell peppers – 4 medium
- Tomatoes (unsweetened, canned) – 4 cups
- Cabbage – 1 medium head

Other Ingredients:

- Pecans, chopped – 60 g
- Almond flour – 500g
- Coconut flour – 200g
- Coconut milk – 2 cans (400ml each)
- Olive oil – 500ml
- Butter – 300g
- Berries (frozen) – 200g
- Walnuts – 100g
- Erythritol sweetener – 200g
- Vanilla extract – 50ml

28 Day Meal Plan / Week 3

Monday

Breakfast p.26	Lunch p.37	Dinner p.37	Snacks p.74
Keto Sausage and Cheese Breakfast Biscuits / (2 biscuits) 400 kcal	Keto Zoodle Chicken Alfredo / (1 serving) 420 kcal	Buffalo Chicken Lettuce Wraps / (1 serving) 280 kcal	Keto Coconut Macaroons / (1 serving) 190 kcal

Total Calories: 1290 kcal | Protein:80g | Fat: 103g | Carbs: 19g

Tuesday

Breakfast p.25	Lunch p.30	Dinner p.43	Snacks p.28
Fluffy Keto Coconut Pancakes / (1 serving) 270 kcal	Low-Carb Broccoli Cheddar Soup / (1 serving) 370 kcal	Keto Balsamic Glazed Pork Loin / (1 serving) 360 kcal	Nut Butter & Berry Parfait /(1 serving) 220 kcal

Total Calories: 1220 kcal | Protein: 67g | Fat: 96 g | Carbs: 22g

Wednesday

Breakfast p.20	Lunch p.42	Dinner p.43	Snacks p.73
Zucchini & Parmesan Egg Frittata / (1 serving) 210 kcal	Keto Sausage and Cabbage Skillet / (1 serving) 370 kcal	Keto Pork Carnitas with Avocado Salsa / (1 serving) 370 kcal	Keto Lemon Bars / (1 serving) 260 kcal

Total Calories: 1210 kcal | Protein: 69g | Fat: 95g | Carbs: 18g

Thursday

Breakfast p.27	Lunch p.37	Dinner p.39	Snacks p.72
Smoked Salmon and Avocado Breakfast Salad / (1 serving) 380 kcal	Keto Chicken Alfredo with Zoodles / (1 serving) 420 kcal	Keto Chicken Parmesan with Almond Flour / (1 serving) 450 kcal	Keto Peanut Butter Chocolate Cups / (1 serving) 260 kcal

Total Calories: 1510 kcal | Protein: 99g | Fat: 114g | Carbs: 21g

Friday

Breakfast p.21	Lunch p.32	Dinner p.43	Snacks p.76
Keto Eggs Benedict with Avocado Hollandaise / (1 serving) 380 kcal	Keto Creamy Bacon and Spinach Salad / (1 serving) 320 kcal	Keto Balsamic Glazed Pork Loin / (1 serving) 360 kcal	Butter Pecan Fat Bombs / (2 bombs) 280 kcal

Total Calories: 1340 kcal | Protein: 65g | Fat: 111g | Carbs: 17g

Saturday

Breakfast p.19	Lunch p.46	Dinner p.48	Snacks p.74
Mushroom and Cheddar Omelet / (1 serving) 340 kcal	Keto Sausage-Stuffed Bell Peppers / (1 serving) 350 kcal	Keto Beef Stroganoff with Zoodles / (1 serving) 370 kcal	Keto Coconut Macaroons /(1 serving) 190 kcal

Total Calories: 1250 kcal | Protein: 84g | Fat: 102g | Carbs: 18g

Sunday

Breakfast p.26	Lunch p.42	Dinner p.34	Snacks p.73
Almond Flour Waffles with Berries / (1 serving) 300 kcal	Keto BBQ Pulled Pork / (1 serving) 370 kcal	Crispy Chicken & Spinach Keto Salad / (1 serving) 350 kcal	Keto Lemon Bars / (1 serving) 260 kcal

Total Calories: 1280 kcal | Protein: 75g | Fat: 100g | Carbs: 20g

28 Day Meal Plan / Week 4

Monday

Breakfast p.18	Lunch p.33	Dinner p.36	Snacks p.72
Avocado Egg Boats / (1 serving) 320 kcal	Tomato Basil Keto Soup / (1 serving) 280 kcal	Bacon-Wrapped Chicken Thighs /(1 serving) 430 kcal	Keto Cheesecake Fat Bombs / (2 fat bombs) 280 kcal

Total Calories: 1310 kcal | Protein: 44g | Fat: 116g | Carbs: 17g

Tuesday

Breakfast p.18	Lunch p.31	Dinner p.56	Snacks p.74
Spinach Egg Cheese Muffins / (2 muffins) 240 kcal	Keto Cream of Mushroom Soup /(1 serving) 330 kcal	Keto Shrimp Alfredo over Zoodles / (1 serving) 420 kcal	Keto Pumpkin Spice Muffins / (1 serving) 280 kcal

Total Calories: 1270 kcal | Protein: 68g | Fat: 104g | Carbs: 17g

Wednesday

Breakfast p.25	Lunch p.31	Dinner p.43	Snacks p.76
Fluffy Keto Coconut Pancakes / (1 serving) 270 kcal	Shrimp and Avocado Keto Caesar Salad /(1 serving) 380 kcal	Keto Pork Carnitas with Avocado Salsa / (1 serving) 370 kcal	Butter Pecan Fat Bombs / (1 serving) 160 kcal

Total Calories: 1180 kcal | Protein: 71g | Fat: 90g | Carbs: 16g

Thursday

Breakfast p.26	Lunch p.32	Dinner p.37	Snacks p.72
Almond Flour Waffles with Butter and Berries / (1 serving) 300 kcal	Spicy Thai Chicken Coconut Soup / (1 serving) 350 kcal	Keto Chicken Alfredo with Zoodles / (1 serving) 450 kcal	Keto Peanut Butter Chocolate Cups / (1 serving) 260 kcal

Total Calories: 1330 kcal | Protein: 74g | Fat: 105 g | Carbs: 23g

Friday

Breakfast p.19	Lunch p.33	Dinner p.42	Snacks p.74
Mushroom and Cheddar Omelet / (1 serving) 340 kcal	Keto Taco Salad / (1 serving) 420 kcal	Keto BBQ Pulled Pork / (1 serving) 370 kcal	Keto Coconut Macaroons /(1 serving) 190 kcal

Total Calories: 1320 kcal | Protein: 85g | Fat: 104g | Carbs: 17g

Saturday

Breakfast p.28	Lunch p.30	Dinner p.34	Snacks p.73
Nut Butter & Berry Breakfast Parfait / (1 serving) 220 kcal	Keto Zoodle Chicken Soup / (1 serving) 350 kcal	Crispy Chicken & Spinach Keto Salad / (1 serving) 350 kcal	Keto Lemon Bars / (1 serving) 260 kcal

Total Calories: 1180 kcal | Protein: 63g | Fat: 92g | Carbs: 23g

Sunday

Breakfast p.27	Lunch p.46	Dinner p.48	Snacks p.27
Smoked Salmon and Avocado Breakfast Salad / (1 serving) 380 kcal	Keto Ham and Cheese Roll-Ups / (1 serving) 370 kcal	Keto Beef Stroganoff with Zoodles / (1 serving) 370 kcal	Keto Cinnamon Rolls / (1 serving) 280 kcal

Total Calories: 1400 kcal | Protein: 100g | Fat: 110g | Carbs: 18g

Chopping List / Week 3 & Week 4

Week 3

Proteins:

- Chicken thighs – 1.5kg
- Ground sausage – 500g
- Pork shoulder – 1kg
- Shrimp – 200g
- Eggs – 18 large
- Smoked salmon – 200g

Dairy:

- Shredded cheddar cheese – 300g
- Heavy cream – 1L
- Parmesan cheese – 300g
- Cream cheese – 100g
- Mozzarella cheese – 200g

Vegetables:

- Avocados – 5 large
- Zucchini – 6 medium
- Bell peppers – 6 medium
- Spinach – 500g
- Broccoli – 300g
- Mushrooms – 200g

Other Ingredients:

- Pecans, chopped – 60 g
- Almond flour – 500g
- Coconut flour – 200g
- Butter – 300g
- Coconut milk – 2 cans (400ml each)
- Olive oil – 500ml
- Berries (frozen) – 200g
- Chia seeds – 100g
- Erythritol sweetener – 200g
- Vanilla extract – 50ml

Week 4

Proteins:

- Chicken thighs – 1.5kg
- Shrimp – 400g
- Ground pork – 500g
- Smoked salmon – 200g
- Eggs – 18 large
- Bacon – 12 slices
- Ground beef – 500g

Dairy:

- Heavy cream – 1L
- Shredded cheddar cheese – 300g
- Cream cheese – 100g
- Parmesan cheese – 200g
- Mozzarella cheese – 200g

Vegetables:

- Avocados – 5 large
- Spinach – 500g
- Zucchini – 6 medium
- Bell peppers – 4 medium
- Broccoli – 300g
- Mushrooms – 200g
- Tomatoes (unsweetened, canned) – 4 cups
- Romaine lettuce – 300g

Other Ingredients:

- Pecans, chopped – 30 g
- Almond flour – 500g
- Coconut flour – 200g
- Butter – 300g
- Coconut milk – 2 cans (400ml each)
- Olive oil – 500ml
- Berries (frozen) – 200g
- Erythritol sweetener – 200g
- Vanilla extract – 50ml

CHAPTER 4

KETO BREAKFASTS WITH EGGS

1. Spinach Egg Cheese Muffins

Servings: 6 muffins • **Prep Time:** 10 minutes • **Cooking Time:** 20 minutes

Ingredients:

- 6 large eggs
- 1 cup fresh spinach, chopped
- 1/2 cup shredded cheddar cheese
- 1/4 cup heavy cream
- 1/4 tsp garlic powder
- 1/4 tsp onion powder
- Salt and pepper to taste
- Optional: 1/4 cup diced cooked bacon or sausage for added flavor

Instructions:

1.Preheat the oven to 350°F (175°C) and grease a muffin tin with non-stick spray or butter. 2.In a large bowl, whisk the eggs and heavy cream together until smooth. 3.Add the chopped spinach, shredded cheddar, garlic powder, onion powder, salt, and pepper. 4.If adding bacon or sausage, fold it in at this point. 5.Pour the mixture evenly into the muffin tin, filling each about 2/3 full. 6.Bake for 18-20 minutes, or until the muffins are set and slightly golden on top. 7.Let cool for a few minutes before removing from the tin.

Chef's Tip: *These muffins freeze well! Make a batch and store them in the freezer. Reheat in the microwave for a quick and easy breakfast.*

Nutrition per Muffin:

- **Calories:** 120
- **Protein:** 8g
- **Carbohydrates:** 1g
- **Fat:** 10g
- **Fiber:** 0g

2. Avocado Egg Boats

Servings: 2 • **Prep Time:** 5 minutes • **Cooking Time:** 15 minutes

Ingredients:

- 2 large ripe avocados, halved and pitted
- 4 large eggs
- 1/4 cup shredded cheddar cheese
- Salt and pepper to taste
- Optional: 2 slices cooked bacon, crumbled
- Optional: 1 tbsp chopped parsley or cilantro for garnish

Instructions:

1.Preheat oven to 400°F (200°C).2.Scoop out a small amount of the avocado flesh to create a larger cavity for the egg.3.Place the avocado halves in a small baking dish, ensuring they are stable.4.Crack an egg into each avocado half, season with salt and pepper, and top with shredded cheddar cheese.5.Bake for 12-15 minutes or until the egg whites are set but the yolks remain runny.6.Garnish with crumbled bacon and chopped parsley, if desired.

Chef's Tip: *For a more even bake, use smaller eggs to avoid overflow in the avocado cavities.*

Nutrition per Serving:

- **Calories:** 320
- **Protein:** 12g
- **Carbohydrates:** 4g
- **Fat:** 28g
- **Fiber:** 7g

3. Creamy Sausage Egg Casserole

Servings: 6 • **Prep Time:** 10 minutes • Cooking **Time:** 30 minutes

Ingredients:

- 8 large eggs
- 1/2 cup heavy cream
- 1 lb ground sausage (sugar-free)
- 1/2 cup shredded cheddar cheese
- 1/4 cup diced onions
- 1/4 cup diced bell peppers
- Salt and pepper to taste
- 1 tbsp butter for greasing

Instructions:

1.Preheat the oven to 350°F (175°C) and grease an 8x8 baking dish with butter.2.In a skillet, cook the ground sausage over medium heat until browned.3. Drain any excess fat.In a large bowl, whisk together the eggs, heavy cream, salt, and pepper.4.Spread the cooked sausage evenly in the greased baking dish, then layer the onions and bell peppers on top.5.Pour the egg mixture over the sausage and vegetables.6. Top with shredded cheddar cheese.

Chef's Tip: *For extra flavor, add a teaspoon of smoked paprika or Italian seasoning to the sausage while it cooks.*

Nutrition per Serving:

- **Calories:** 380
- **Protein:** 20g
- **Carbohydrates:** 2g
- **Fat:** 32g
- **Fiber:** 0g

4. Mushroom and Cheddar Omelet

Servings: 1 • **Prep Time:** 5 minutes • Cooking **Time:** 7 minutes

Ingredients:

- 3 large eggs
- 1/2 cup mushrooms, sliced
- 1/4 cup shredded cheddar cheese
- 1 tbsp butter
- Salt and pepper to taste
- Optional: 1 tsp fresh chives, chopped for garnish

Instructions:

1.Heat 1/2 tbsp butter in a non-stick skillet over medium heat. Add the sliced mushrooms and sauté until softened, about 3 minutes. Set aside.2.In a small bowl, whisk the eggs with a pinch of salt and pepper.3.Add the remaining butter to the skillet, then pour the egg mixture in and let it cook for 1-2 minutes until the edges begin to set.4.Add the sautéed mushrooms and shredded cheddar cheese to one half of the omelet. Fold the other half over and cook for an additional 1-2 minutes until the cheese is melted and the eggs are fully cooked.5.Slide the omelet onto a plate and garnish with fresh chives, if desired.

Chef's Tip: *For added creaminess, whisk in 1 tbsp of heavy cream with the eggs before cooking.*

Nutrition per Serving:

- **Calories:** 340
- **Protein:** 20g
- **Carbohydrates:** 3g
- **Fat:** 28g
- **Fiber:** 1g

5. Zucchini & Parmesan Egg Frittata

Servings: 4• **Prep Time:** 10 minutes • Cooking **Time:** 20 minutes

Ingredients:

- 6 large eggs
- 1 medium zucchini, thinly sliced
- 1/2 cup grated Parmesan cheese
- 1/4 cup heavy cream
- 1/4 tsp garlic powder
- 1 tbsp butter
- Salt and pepper to taste
- Optional: Fresh basil or parsley for garnish

Instructions:

1.Preheat oven to 375°F (190°C).2. In a bowl, whisk together the eggs, heavy cream, garlic powder, salt, and pepper.3. Heat butter in an oven-safe skillet over medium heat. Add the zucchini slices and sauté until softened, about 3-4 minutes.4. Pour the egg mixture over the zucchini and sprinkle Parmesan cheese evenly on top.5. Cook on the stovetop for 2-3 minutes, then transfer the skillet to the preheated oven. Bake for 10-12 minutes, or until the frittata is set and golden.6. Remove from the oven and let cool slightly before slicing.

Chef's Tip: *For extra flavor, add a handful of fresh herbs like basil or parsley before baking.*

Nutrition per Serving:

- **Calories:** 210
- **Protein:** 12g
- **Carbohydrates:** 3g
- **Fat:** 17g
- **Fiber:** 1g

6.Bacon-Wrapped Egg Cups

Servings: 6 egg cups • **Prep Time:** 10 minutes • Cooking **Time:** 20 minutes

Ingredients:

- 6 large eggs
- 6 slices of bacon
- 1/4 cup shredded cheddar cheese
- 1/4 tsp garlic powder
- Salt and pepper to taste
- Optional: chopped chives or parsley for garnish

Instructions:

1.Preheat oven to 375°F (190°C). Grease a 6-cup muffin tin.2.Partially cook the bacon in a skillet over medium heat for 3-4 minutes, just until it starts to crisp but is still pliable.3.Line each muffin cup with a slice of bacon, wrapping it around the sides.4.Crack an egg into each bacon-lined cup, season with salt, pepper, and garlic powder, and sprinkle a little cheddar cheese on top.5.Bake for 15-18 minutes, or until the eggs are set to your desired doneness.6.Let cool for a few minutes before removing from the muffin tin. Garnish with chopped chives or parsley, if desired.

Chef's Tip: *For runnier yolks, bake the egg cups for a shorter time and check the eggs frequently.*

Nutrition per Egg Cup:

- **Calories:** 180
- **Protein:** 10g
- **Carbohydrates:** 1g
- **Fat:** 15g
- **Fiber:** 0g

7. Spanish-Style Egg and Chorizo Skillet

Servings: 4 • **Prep Time:** 10 minutes • **Cooking Time:** 15 minutes

Ingredients:

- 6 large eggs
- 1/2 lb chorizo sausage, sliced
- 1/2 cup diced bell peppers (red or green)
- 1/4 cup diced onions
- 1/4 cup diced tomatoes
- 2 tbsp olive oil
- 1 tsp smoked paprika
- Salt and pepper to taste
- Optional: Fresh cilantro for garnish

Instructions:

1.Heat olive oil in a large skillet over medium heat. Add the chorizo and cook until browned, about 5 minutes.2. Add the diced onions, bell peppers, and tomatoes to the skillet. Cook for another 3-4 minutes until softened.3. In a separate bowl, whisk together the eggs, smoked paprika, salt, and pepper.4. Pour the egg mixture over the chorizo and vegetables in the skillet. Stir gently to combine.5. Cook until the eggs are scrambled and fully set, about 5 minutes. Stir occasionally to prevent sticking.6. Garnish with fresh cilantro if desired.

Nutrition per Serving:

- **Calories:** 310
- **Protein:** 18g
- **Carbohydrates:** 3g
- **Fat:** 25g
- **Fiber:** 1g

Chef's Tip: *For a bit of heat, add a pinch of red pepper flakes to the egg mixture before cooking.*

8. Keto Eggs Benedict with Avocado

Servings: 2 • **Prep Time:** 10 minutes • **Cooking Time:** 10 minutes

Ingredients:

- 4 large eggs
- 2 slices of Canadian bacon (or regular bacon)
- 2 slices of keto-friendly bread (optional)
- 1 ripe avocado
- 2 tbsp lemon juice
- 1/4 cup butter, melted
- Salt and pepper to taste
- Optional: chopped parsley for garnish

Instructions:

1.In a skillet, cook the bacon until crispy and set aside.2. In a pot, bring water to a gentle simmer for poaching the eggs. Crack each egg into a small bowl, then carefully slide it into the simmering water. Poach for 3-4 minutes, or until the whites are set but the yolks are still runny.3. In a blender, combine the avocado, lemon juice, and melted butter. Blend until smooth and creamy. Add salt and pepper to taste.4. If using keto bread, lightly toast the slices. Place a slice of bacon on each piece of bread.5. Top with the poached eggs and drizzle with the avocado hollandaise sauce.6. Garnish with chopped parsley if desired.

Nutrition per Serving:

- **Calories:** 380
- **Protein:** 16g
- **Carbohydrates:** 5g
- **Fat:** 33g
- **Fiber:** 3g

Chef's Tip: *For an extra smooth hollandaise, strain the avocado mixture through a fine mesh sieve before serving.*

9.Egg-Stuffed Keto Breakfast Peppers

Servings: 2 • **Prep Time:** 10 minutes • Cooking **Time:** 20 minutes

Ingredients:

- 2 medium bell peppers, halved and seeded
- 4 large eggs
- 1/4 cup shredded mozzarella cheese
- 2 tbsp heavy cream
- 1/4 tsp garlic powder
- Salt and pepper to taste
- Optional: Fresh parsley for garnish

Instructions:

1.Preheat the oven to 375°F (190°C).2.Place the halved bell peppers in a baking dish, cut side up.3.In a small bowl, whisk together the eggs, heavy cream, garlic powder, salt, and pepper.4.Pour the egg mixture into each bell pepper half, filling them about 3/4 of the way full.5.Sprinkle shredded mozzarella cheese on top.6.Bake for 18-20 minutes, or until the eggs are fully set and the peppers are tender.7.Garnish with fresh parsley before serving, if desired.

Chef's Tip: *For extra flavor, add crumbled bacon or cooked sausage into the bell pepper before pouring in the egg mixture.*

Nutrition per Serving:

- **Calories:** 280
- **Protein:** 16g
- **Carbohydrates:** 6g
- **Fat:** 22g
- **Fiber:** 2g

10. Keto Egg Salad with Dill and Avocado

Servings: 4 • **Prep Time:** 10 minutes •

Ingredients:

- 6 large hard-boiled eggs, chopped
- 1 ripe avocado, diced
- 1/4 cup mayonnaise
- 1 tbsp fresh dill, chopped
- 1 tbsp lemon juice
- 1/4 tsp garlic powder
- Salt and pepper to taste
- Optional: Romaine lettuce leaves for serving

Instructions:

1.In a large mixing bowl, combine the chopped eggs, diced avocado, and mayonnaise.2. Add the fresh dill, lemon juice, garlic powder, salt, and pepper. Gently mix until everything is well combined.3.Serve as a salad on its own, or scoop the egg salad into romaine lettuce leaves for a low-carb wrap.

Chef's Tip: *Use a fork to gently mash the avocado into the salad for a creamy texture, but leave some chunks for added flavor.*

Nutrition per Serving:

- **Calories:** 280
- **Protein:** 10g
- **Carbohydrates:** 4g
- **Fat:** 24g
- **Fiber:** 3g

CHAPTER 5

BREAKFASTS WITHOUT EGGS

1. Keto Vanilla Chia Pudding

<u>**Servings:**</u> 2 • <u>**Prep Time:**</u> 5 minutes • <u>**Chill Time:**</u> 2 hours or overnight

Ingredients:
- 1 cup unsweetened almond milk
- 2 tbsp chia seeds
- 1/2 tsp vanilla extract
- 1 tbsp erythritol or another keto-friendly sweetener (optional)
- 1 tbsp heavy cream (optional for creaminess)

Instructions:

1.In a medium bowl, combine the almond milk, chia seeds, vanilla extract, and sweetener (if using).2.Stir the mixture well, making sure the chia seeds are evenly distributed.3.Let the mixture sit for 5 minutes, then stir again to prevent clumping.4.Cover the bowl and refrigerate for at least 2 hours or overnight until the chia seeds absorb the liquid and the pudding thickens.5.For extra creaminess, stir in heavy cream before serving.

Chef's Tip: *For added flavor, top the pudding with a few raspberries or a sprinkle of unsweetened shredded coconut.*

Nutrition per Serving:
- **Calories:** 130
- **Protein:** 3g
- **Carbohydrates:** 4g
- **Fat:** 11g
- **Fiber:** 3g

2. Low-Carb Berry Almond Smoothie

<u>**Servings:**</u> 1 • <u>**Prep Time:**</u> 5 minutes

Ingredients:
- 1/2 cup unsweetened almond
- milk
- 1/4 cup frozen berries
- (raspberries, blackberries,
- or strawberries)
- 1 tbsp almond butter
- 1/4 cup heavy cream
- 1 tbsp chia seeds
- 1-2 tbsp erythritol or stevia (to taste)
- 1/4 tsp vanilla extract
- Optional: Ice cubes for a thicker texture

Instructions:

1.Add the almond milk, frozen berries, almond butter, heavy cream, chia seeds, sweetener, and vanilla extract to a blender.
2.Blend on high until smooth and creamy. If a thicker consistency is desired, add a few ice cubes and blend again.
3.Pour into a glass and enjoy immediately.

Chef's Tip: *Use frozen berries to achieve a thicker smoothie, and adjust the sweetness to taste with keto-friendly sweeteners.*

Nutrition per Serving:
- **Calories:** 260
- **Protein:** 4g
- **Carbohydrates:** 7g
- **Fat:** 24g
- **Fiber:** 4g

3. Fluffy Keto Coconut Pancakes

Servings: 2 • **Prep Time:** 5 minutes • **Cooking Time:** 10 minutes

Ingredients:
- 1/4 cup coconut flour
- 2 large eggs
- 1/4 cup heavy cream
- 1/4 cup unsweetened almond milk
- 1/2 tsp baking powder
- 1/2 tsp vanilla extract
- 1 tbsp erythritol or another keto sweetener (optional)
- 1 tbsp melted butter (for cooking)

Instructions:

1. In a medium bowl, whisk together the eggs, heavy cream, almond milk, vanilla extract, and sweetener.
2. Gradually add the coconut flour and baking powder, whisking until smooth. Let the batter rest for 2-3 minutes to thicken.
3. Heat butter in a non-stick skillet over medium-low heat.
4. Pour 2-3 tbsp of batter onto the skillet for each pancake. Cook for 2-3 minutes on each side, until golden brown and cooked through.
5. Serve warm with butter or sugar-free syrup.

Chef's Tip: *For fluffier pancakes, add 1/4 tsp of baking soda and a splash of lemon juice to the batter just before cooking.*

Nutrition per Serving:
- **Calories:** 270
- **Protein:** 10g
- **Carbohydrates:** 6g
- **Fat:** 24g
- **Fiber:** 4g

4. Keto "Oatmeal" with Cinnamon and Walnuts

Servings: 1 • **Prep Time:** 5 minutes • **Cooking Time:** 5 minutes

Ingredients:
- 2 tbsp ground flaxseeds
- 2 tbsp chia seeds
- 1/4 cup unsweetened
- almond milk
- 1/4 cup water
- 1 tbsp coconut flour
- 1 tbsp heavy cream
- 1/2 tsp cinnamon
- 1 tbsp walnuts, chopped
- 1-2 tbsp erythritol or stevia (optional)
- Optional: A splash of vanilla extract or butter

Instructions:

1. In a small saucepan, combine the flaxseeds, chia seeds, almond milk, water, coconut flour, and cinnamon. Cook over medium heat, stirring constantly, for about 3-5 minutes, until the mixture thickens to an oatmeal-like consistency. 2. Stir in the heavy cream and sweetener, if desired. 3. Remove from heat and top with chopped walnuts. Optionally, add a splash of vanilla extract or a small pat of butter for extra flavor. 4. Serve warm.

Chef's Tip: *For a creamier texture, substitute almond milk with coconut milk, and let the "oatmeal" rest for a few minutes to absorb the liquid fully before serving.*

Nutrition per Serving:
- **Calories:** 290
- **Protein:** 8g
- **Carbohydrates:** 7g
- **Fat:** 25g
- **Fiber:** 6g

5. Almond Flour Waffles with Butter and Berries

Servings: 2 • **Prep Time:** 5 minutes • Cooking **Time:** 10 minutes

Ingredients:

- 1/2 cup almond flour
- 2 large eggs
- 2 tbsp melted butter
- (plus more for serving)
- 1/4 cup unsweetened
- almond milk
- 1/2 tsp baking powder
- 1/2 tsp vanilla extract
- 1-2 tbsp erythritol or stevia (optional)
- 1/4 cup fresh berries (raspberries or blueberries)
- Optional: sugar-free syrup for serving

Nutrition per Serving:

- **Calories:** 300
- **Protein:** 10g
- **Carbohydrates:** 6g
- **Fat:** 26g
- **Fiber:** 4g

Instructions:

1. Preheat the waffle iron and grease it with non-stick spray or butter.
2. In a medium bowl, whisk together the almond flour, eggs, melted butter, almond milk, baking powder, vanilla extract, and sweetener (if using).
3. Pour the batter into the preheated waffle iron and cook according to the manufacturer's instructions, about 3-5 minutes per batch. 4. Serve warm with a pat of butter, fresh berries, and optional sugar-free syrup.

Chef's Tip: *For an extra crispy texture, cook the waffles slightly longer until golden brown.*

6. Keto Sausage and Cheese Breakfast Biscuits

Servings: 6 biscuits • **Prep Time:** 10 minutes • Cooking **Time:** 20 minutes

Ingredients:

- 1 cup almond flour
- 1/2 cup shredded cheddar cheese
- 1/4 cup cooked sausage crumbles (sugar-free)
- 1/4 cup sour cream
- 1 large egg
- 1 tsp baking powder
- 1/4 tsp garlic powder
- Salt and pepper to taste

Nutrition per Biscuit:

- **Calories:** 200
- **Protein:** 8g
- **Carbohydrates:** 3g
- **Fat:** 18g
- **Fiber:** 2g

Instructions:

1. Preheat the oven to 350°F (175°C) and line a baking sheet with parchment paper. 2. In a large bowl, mix together almond flour, cheddar cheese, sausage crumbles, garlic powder, baking powder, salt, and pepper.
3. In a separate bowl, whisk together the egg and sour cream. Add the wet ingredients to the dry ingredients and stir until combined.
4. Scoop the dough onto the baking sheet in 6 even portions.
5. Bake for 18-20 minutes, or until the biscuits are golden and firm to the touch. 6. Let cool slightly before serving.

Chef's Tip: *Add a pinch of smoked paprika or cayenne pepper for extra flavor.*

7. Smoked Salmon and Avocado Breakfast Salad

<u>Servings:</u> 2 • <u>Prep Time:</u> 10 minutes

Ingredients:

- 4 oz smoked salmon
- 1 large avocado, diced
- 2 cups mixed greens
- 2 hard-boiled eggs, sliced
- 1/4 cup cucumber, diced
- 2 tbsp olive oil
- 1 tbsp lemon juice
- Salt and pepper to taste
- Optional: 1 tbsp capers or fresh dill for garnish

Instructions:

1.In a large bowl, toss the mixed greens, diced avocado, and cucumber.
2.Drizzle with olive oil and lemon juice, then season with salt and pepper.
3.Top the salad with smoked salmon slices and hard-boiled egg slices.
4.Garnish with capers or fresh dill, if desired.

Chef's Tip: *For a heartier meal, add a dollop of sour cream or cream cheese on top of the salad.*

Nutrition per Serving:

- **Calories:** 380
- **Protein:** 18g
- **Carbohydrates:** 5g
- **Fat:** 32g
- **Fiber:** 4g

8. Keto-Friendly Cinnamon Rolls

<u>Servings:</u> 6 rolls • **Prep Time:** 15 minutes • Cooking **Time:** 25 minutes

Ingredients:

For the dough:
- 2 cups shredded
- mozzarella cheese
- 2 oz cream cheese
- 1 cup almond flour
- 1 large egg
- 1 tsp baking powder
- 1/2 tsp vanilla extract

For the filling:
- 2 tbsp melted butter
- 2 tbsp erythritol or other keto sweetener
- 1 tbsp cinnamon

For the icing:
- 2 oz cream cheese, softened
- 1/4 cup powdered erythritol
- 1 tbsp heavy cream
- 1/4 tsp vanilla extract

Instructions:

1.Preheat the oven to 350°F (175°C) and grease a baking dish.2.In a microwave-safe bowl, melt the mozzarella and cream cheese together in 30-second intervals, stirring until smooth.3.In another bowl, mix the almond flour, baking powder, and egg, then add to the melted cheese mixture. Knead until a dough forms.4.Roll the dough out between two sheets of parchment paper into a rectangle about 1/4 inch thick.5.Brush the melted butter over the dough and sprinkle with erythritol and cinnamon. 6.Roll the dough into a log and slice into 6 even pieces. Place the rolls in the prepared baking dish.7.Bake for 20-25 minutes or until golden brown.8.While the rolls bake, prepare the icing by whisking together the cream cheese, powdered erythritol, heavy cream, and vanilla extract.9.Drizzle the icing over the warm cinnamon rolls before serving.

Chef's Tip: *For a softer dough, let the dough rest for a few minutes after kneading. It will firm up slightly, making it easier to work with.*

Nutrition per Serving:

- **Calories:** 280
- **Protein:** 12g
- **Carbohydrates:** 5g
- **Fat:** 24g
- **Fiber:** 2g

9. Nut Butter & Berry Breakfast Parfait

<u>**Servings:**</u> 2 • <u>**Prep Time:**</u> 5 minutes

Ingredients:
- 1/2 cup unsweetened Greek yogurt or coconut yogurt
- 2 tbsp almond butter or peanut butter
- 1/4 cup fresh raspberries or blackberries
- 1 tbsp chia seeds
- 1 tbsp unsweetened shredded coconut
- Optional: A drizzle of sugar-free syrup
-

Instructions:

1. In two small bowls or parfait glasses, layer half of the yogurt, almond butter, and fresh berries.
2. Sprinkle with chia seeds and shredded coconut.
3. Repeat the layers with the remaining ingredients.
4. If desired, drizzle with sugar-free syrup.
5. Serve immediately or refrigerate for later.

Chef's Tip: *Add a pinch of cinnamon or a few crushed nuts on top for added crunch and flavor.*

Nutrition per Serving:
- **Calories:** 220
- **Protein:** 8g
- **Carbohydrates:** 7g
- **Fat:** 18g
- **Fiber:** 5g

10. Savory Keto Bacon and Cheese Muffins

<u>**Servings:**</u> 6 muffins • <u>**Prep Time:**</u> 10 minutes • Cooking **Time:** 20 minutes

Ingredients:
- 1 cup almond flour
- 1/2 cup shredded cheddar cheese
- 4 slices bacon, cooked and crumbled
- 1/4 cup sour cream
- 2 large eggs
- 1 tsp baking powder
- 1/4 tsp garlic powder
- 1/4 tsp salt
- Optional: Chopped chives for garnish

Instructions:

1. Preheat the oven to 350°F (175°C) and grease a 6-cup muffin tin.
2. In a large bowl, whisk together almond flour, baking powder, garlic powder, and salt.3. In a separate bowl, whisk the eggs and sour cream, then add to the dry ingredients. Stir in the cheddar cheese and crumbled bacon.
4. Divide the batter evenly between the muffin cups.
5. Bake for 18-20 minutes, or until the muffins are golden brown and firm.
6. Allow the muffins to cool slightly before serving. Garnish with chopped chives if desired.

Chef's Tip: *For a crispier muffin top, sprinkle a little extra shredded cheddar cheese on top of the muffins before baking.*

Nutrition per Muffin:
- **Calories:** 230
- **Protein:** 10g
- **Carbohydrates:** 3g
- **Fat:** 20g
- **Fiber:** 2g

CHAPTER 6

KETO SOUPS AND SALADS

1. Keto Chicken Zoodle Soup

Servings: 4 • **Prep Time:** 10 minutes • Cooking **Time:** 20 minutes

Ingredients:
- 1 lb chicken breast, cooked and shredded
- 2 medium zucchini, spiralized into zoodles
- 4 cups chicken broth
- 1/2 cup heavy cream
- 1/4 cup diced onions
- 2 tbsp butter
- 1 clove garlic, minced
- 1/2 tsp dried thyme
- 1/2 tsp dried parsley
- Salt and pepper to taste
- Optional: Fresh parsley for garnish

Instructions:
1.In a large pot, melt the butter over medium heat. Add the diced onions and garlic, sautéing until softened, about 3-4 minutes.2. Add the chicken broth, thyme, parsley, salt, and pepper. Bring the mixture to a boil, then reduce the heat and simmer for 10 minutes.3. Stir in the heavy cream and shredded chicken. Simmer for an additional 5 minutes until heated through.4. Just before serving, add the zucchini noodles (zoodles) and cook for 2-3 minutes until they are slightly tender but still firm.5.Serve hot, garnished with fresh parsley if desired.

Chef's Tip: *To avoid soggy zoodles, add them to the soup just before serving.*

Nutrition per Serving:
- **Calories:** 350
- **Protein:** 26g
- **Carbohydrates:** 5g
- **Fat:** 24g
- **Fiber:** 1g

2. Low-Carb Broccoli Cheddar Soup

Servings: 4 • **Prep Time:** 10 minutes • Cooking **Time:** 20 minutes

Ingredients:
- 4 cups broccoli florets
- 2 cups chicken broth
- 1 cup heavy cream
- 1 1/2 cups shredded cheddar cheese
- 1/4 cup grated Parmesan cheese
- 2 tbsp butter
- 1/2 tsp garlic powder
- 1/2 tsp onion powder
- Salt and pepper to taste
- Optional: Crumbled bacon or extra cheese for garnish

Instructions:
1.In a large pot, melt the butter over medium heat. Add the broccoli florets and sauté for 3-4 minutes.2. Add the chicken broth, garlic powder, and onion powder. Bring to a boil, then reduce heat and simmer for 10-12 minutes until the broccoli is tender.3. Use an immersion blender to blend the soup to your desired consistency (smooth or chunky). Alternatively, transfer to a blender and blend until smooth.4. Stir in the heavy cream, cheddar cheese, Parmesan cheese, salt, and pepper. Stir until the cheese is fully melted and the soup is creamy.5. Serve hot, garnished with crumbled bacon or extra cheese if desired.

Chef's Tip: *For a thicker consistency, blend only half of the soup, leaving some broccoli chunks for texture.*

Nutrition per Serving:
- **Calories:** 370
- **Protein:** 14g
- **Carbohydrates:** 6g
- **Fat:** 32g
- **Fiber:** 3g

3. Keto Cream of Mushroom Soup

Servings: 4 • **Prep Time:** 10 minutes • **Cooking Time:** 20 minutes

Ingredients:

- 2 cups sliced mushrooms (button or cremini)
- 1 1/2 cups chicken broth
- 1 cup heavy cream
- 1/2 cup grated Parmesan cheese
- 2 tbsp butter
- 1 clove garlic, minced
- 1/2 tsp dried thyme
- Salt and pepper to taste
- Optional: Fresh thyme for garnish

Instructions:

1.In a large pot, melt the butter over medium heat. Add the mushrooms and garlic, sautéing until the mushrooms are tender, about 5 minutes.2. Stir in the chicken broth, thyme, salt, and pepper. Bring to a boil, then reduce heat and simmer for 10 minutes.3. Use an immersion blender to blend the soup to your desired consistency, leaving some mushroom chunks if you prefer a chunkier texture.4.Stir in the heavy cream and Parmesan cheese. Simmer for an additional 5 minutes until the soup is creamy and thick.5. Serve hot, garnished with fresh thyme if desired.

Chef's Tip: *For a richer soup, add a splash of dry white wine while sautéing the mushrooms.*

Nutrition per Serving:

- **Calories:** 330
- **Protein:** 9g
- **Carbohydrates:** 5g
- **Fat:** 30g
- **Fiber:** 1g

4. Shrimp and Avocado Keto Caesar Salad

Servings: 2 • **Prep Time:** 10 minutes • **Cooking Time:** 10 minutes

Ingredients:

- 12 large shrimp, peeled and deveined
- 1 tbsp olive oil
- 1 ripe avocado, diced
- 4 cups romaine lettuce, chopped
- 1/4 cup grated Parmesan cheese
- 1/4 cup keto Caesar dressing
- 1 tsp garlic powder
- Salt and pepper to taste
- Optional: Lemon wedges for garnish

Instructions:

1.Heat olive oil in a skillet over medium heat. Season the shrimp with garlic powder, salt, and pepper, then cook for 2-3 minutes on each side until opaque and fully cooked. Set aside.
2.In a large bowl, toss the romaine lettuce with the keto Caesar dressing.
3.Top the salad with cooked shrimp, diced avocado, and Parmesan cheese.
4.Serve with lemon wedges for extra tang if desired.

Chef's Tip: *For added flavor, grill the shrimp instead of pan-frying.*

Nutrition per Serving:

- **Calories:** 380
- **Protein:** 25g
- **Carbohydrates:** 6g
- **Fat:** 28g
- **Fiber:** 4g

5. Spicy Thai Chicken Coconut Soup

<u>Servings:</u> 4 • <u>Prep Time:</u> 10 minutes • <u>Cooking Time:</u> 20 minutes

Ingredients:

- 1 lb chicken breast, thinly sliced
- 4 cups chicken broth
- 1 can (13.5 oz) full-fat coconut milk
- 1 tbsp red curry paste
- 1 tbsp fish sauce
- 1 tbsp lime juice
- 1 tsp ginger, minced
- 1 tbsp olive oil
- 1/2 cup mushrooms, sliced
- 1/2 cup red bell pepper, sliced
- 1/4 cup fresh cilantro for garnish
- Optional: Red pepper flakes for extra heat

Instructions:

1.Heat olive oil in a large pot over medium heat. Add ginger and curry paste, sautéing for 1-2 minutes until fragrant.2. Add the chicken broth and coconut milk, stirring to combine. Bring to a simmer.3. Add the chicken, mushrooms, red bell pepper, fish sauce, and lime juice. Simmer for 10-12 minutes until the chicken is fully cooked.4. Serve hot, garnished with fresh cilantro and red pepper flakes if desired.

Chef's Tip: *For a richer flavor, use boneless chicken thighs instead of chicken breast.*

Nutrition per Serving:

- **Calories:** 350
- **Protein:** 25g
- **Carbohydrates:** 6g
- **Fat:** 25g
- **Fiber:** 1g

6. Creamy Spinach and Bacon Salad

<u>Servings:</u> 2 • <u>Prep Time:</u> 10 minutes • <u>Cooking Time:</u> 10 minutes

Ingredients:

- 4 cups fresh spinach
- 4 slices of bacon, cooked and crumbled
- 1/4 cup sour cream
- 2 tbsp mayonnaise
- 1 tsp Dijon mustard
- 1/4 tsp garlic powder
- 1 hard-boiled egg, chopped
- Salt and pepper to taste

Instructions:

1.Cook the bacon in a skillet until crispy, then crumble and set aside.
2.In a small bowl, whisk together the sour cream, mayonnaise, Dijon mustard, garlic powder, salt, and pepper.
3.In a large bowl, toss the spinach with the dressing until evenly coated.
4.Top the salad with crumbled bacon and chopped hard-boiled egg.

Chef's Tip: *For a warm spinach salad, pour the bacon fat from the skillet over the spinach and toss before adding the dressing.*

Nutrition per Serving:

- **Calories:** 320
- **Protein:** 10g
- **Carbohydrates:** 5g
- **Fat:** 28g
- **Fiber:** 2g

7. Tomato Basil Keto Soup

Servings: 4 • **Prep Time:** 10 minutes • **Cooking Time:** 20 minutes

Ingredients:

- 4 cups canned diced tomatoes (unsweetened)
- 1 cup heavy cream
- 2 cups chicken or vegetable broth
- 1/4 cup olive oil
- 1/4 cup fresh basil leaves, chopped
- 1/2 tsp garlic powder
- 1/2 tsp onion powder
- Salt and pepper to taste
- Optional: Parmesan cheese for garnish

Instructions:

1.In a large pot, heat the olive oil over medium heat. Add the garlic powder and onion powder, stirring for 1 minute.2. Add the diced tomatoes and broth. Bring the mixture to a boil, then reduce heat and simmer for 15 minutes.3.Use an immersion blender to blend the soup until smooth (or blend in batches in a regular blender).4.Stir in the heavy cream and fresh basil. Season with salt and pepper to taste.
5.Simmer for another 5 minutes, then serve hot with a sprinkle of Parmesan cheese if desired.

Chef's Tip: *For extra flavor, roast the tomatoes in the oven for 15 minutes before adding them to the soup.*

Nutrition per Serving:

- **Calories:** 280
- **Protein:** 4g
- **Carbohydrates:** 8g
- **Fat:** 24g
- **Fiber:** 2g

8. Creamy Keto Taco Salad

Servings: 4 • **Prep Time:** 10 minutes • **Cooking Time:** 15 minutes

Ingredients:

- 1 lb ground beef
- 2 tbsp olive oil
- 1 tbsp taco seasoning (keto-friendly)
- 1/2 cup shredded cheddar cheese
- 1/2 cup sour cream
- 1/4 cup salsa (sugar-free)
- 4 cups romaine lettuce, chopped
- 1 ripe avocado, diced
- Optional: Fresh cilantro for garnish

Instructions:

1.In a skillet, heat the olive oil over medium heat. Add the ground beef and cook until browned, about 8-10 minutes.
2.Stir in the taco seasoning and cook for an additional 2-3 minutes. Set aside.
3.In a large bowl, combine the romaine lettuce, avocado, cheddar cheese, sour cream, and salsa.
4.Add the seasoned ground beef to the salad and toss everything together.
5.Serve with fresh cilantro if desired.

Chef's Tip: *For added crunch, top the salad with crushed pork rinds instead of tortilla chips.*

Nutrition per Serving:

- **Calories:** 420
- **Protein:** 25g
- **Carbohydrates:** 6g
- **Fat:** 34g
- **Fiber:** 4g

9. Classic Keto Caesar Salad

Servings: 4 • **Prep Time:** 10 minutes

Ingredients:

- 6 cups (300 g) romaine lettuce,
- chopped
- 1/2 cup (50 g) freshly grated Parmesan cheese
- 1/4 cup (60 ml) olive oil
- 1/4 cup (60 g) mayonnaise
- 1 tbsp (15 ml) lemon juice
- 1 tsp Dijon mustard
- 1 tsp Worcestershire sauce
- 1 clove garlic, minced
- Salt and pepper to taste
- 2 oz (56 g) cooked bacon, crumbled (optional)

Instructions:

1. In a small bowl, whisk together olive oil, mayonnaise, lemon juice, mustard, Worcestershire sauce, garlic, salt, and pepper to make the dressing.
2. In a large bowl, toss the chopped romaine with the grated Parmesan.
3. Pour the dressing over the salad and toss well to coat.
4. Top with crumbled bacon if using.
5. Serve immediately.

Chef's Tip: *For extra crunch, add keto-friendly croutons made from almond flour bread or cheese crisps.*

Nutrition per Serving:

- **Calories**: 290
- **Protein**: 6 g
- **Carbohydrates**: 4 g
- **Fat**: 28 g
- **Fiber**: 2 g

10. Crispy Chicken & Spinach Keto Salad

Servings: 4 • **Prep Time:** 10 minutes • **Cooking Time:** 15 minutes

Ingredients:

- 2 boneless, skinless chicken
- breasts (300 g), cooked
- and shredded
- 4 cups (200 g) fresh
- spinach leaves
- 1/4 cup (60 ml) olive oil
- 1 tbsp (15 ml) apple cider vinegar
- 1 tsp Dijon mustard
- Salt and pepper to taste
- 1/2 cup (56 g) Parmesan crisps, crumbled
- 1/4 cup (30 g) sunflower seeds

Instructions:

1. Heat a skillet over medium heat and cook the chicken breasts until golden brown and cooked through, about 6-8 minutes per side. Once cool, shred the chicken.2.In a small bowl, whisk together olive oil, apple cider vinegar, mustard, salt, and pepper to make the dressing.3.In a large bowl, toss the spinach with the shredded chicken, Parmesan crisps, and sunflower seeds.4.Drizzle with the dressing and toss to combine.5.Serve immediately.

Chef's Tip: *For extra crunch and flavor, cook the chicken in bacon fat or ghee instead of olive oil.*

Nutrition per Serving:

- **Calories**: 350
- **Protein**: 25 g
- **Carbohydrates**: 5 g
- **Fat**: 26 g
- **Fiber**: 2 g

CHAPTER 7
POULTRY RECIPES

1. Bacon-Wrapped Chicken Thighs

__Servings:__ 4 • __Prep Time:__ 10 minutes • __Cooking Time:__ 35 minutes

Ingredients:

- 4 boneless, skinless chicken thighs
- 8 slices of bacon
- 1 tsp garlic powder
- 1 tsp smoked paprika
- 1/2 tsp black pepper
- 1/2 tsp salt
- 1 tbsp olive oil

Instructions:

1.Preheat the oven to 400°F (200°C).2. In a small bowl, mix garlic powder, smoked paprika, black pepper, and salt. Rub the seasoning evenly over the chicken thighs.3. Wrap each chicken thigh with 2 slices of bacon, securing with toothpicks if necessary.4. Heat olive oil in an ovenproof skillet over medium heat. Sear the bacon-wrapped chicken thighs for 3-4 minutes on each side until the bacon is crispy.5. Transfer the skillet to the preheated oven and bake for 25-30 minutes until the chicken is fully cooked.6. Let the chicken rest for 5 minutes before serving.

__Chef's Tip:__ *Serve with a side of roasted vegetables or cauliflower mash for a complete keto meal.*

Nutrition per Serving:

- __Calories:__ 430
- __Protein:__ 24g
- __Carbohydrates:__ 1g
- __Fat:__ 36g
- __Fiber:__ 0g

2. Garlic Parmesan Keto Chicken Wings

__Servings:__ 4 • __Prep Time:__ 10 minutes • __Cooking Time:__ 40 minutes

Ingredients:

- 2 lbs chicken wings
- 1/4 cup olive oil
- 1/4 cup grated Parmesan cheese
- 2 tbsp butter, melted
- 2 tbsp minced garlic
- 1 tsp garlic powder
- 1/2 tsp smoked paprika
- 1/2 tsp salt
- 1/4 tsp black pepper
- Optional: Fresh parsley for garnish

Instructions:

1.Preheat the oven to 400°F (200°C) and line a baking sheet with parchment paper.2.In a large bowl, toss the chicken wings with olive oil, garlic powder, smoked paprika, salt, and pepper until evenly coated. 3.Spread the wings out on the baking sheet and bake for 35-40 minutes, flipping halfway through, until crispy and golden.4.While the wings bake, melt the butter in a small saucepan over medium heat. Stir in the minced garlic and cook for 1-2 minutes until fragrant. Remove from heat and stir in the grated Parmesan.5.Toss the cooked wings in the garlic Parmesan sauce and garnish with fresh parsley if desired.

__Chef's Tip:__ *For extra crispiness, broil the wings for the last 2-3 minutes of baking.*

Nutrition per Serving:

- __Calories:__ 390
- __Protein:__ 26g
- __Carbohydrates:__ 2g
- __Fat:__ 32g
- __Fiber:__ 0g

3. Keto Chicken Alfredo with Zoodles

Servings: 4 • **Prep Time:** 10 minutes • **Cooking Time:** 20 minutes

Ingredients:

- 4 boneless, skinless chicken
- breasts, sliced
- 4 medium zucchini,
- spiralized into zoodles
- 1 cup heavy cream
- 1/2 cup Parmesan cheese,
- grated
- 2 tbsp butter
- 1 tbsp olive oil
- 1/2 tsp garlic powder
- 1/2 tsp Italian seasoning
- Salt and pepper to taste
- Optional: Fresh parsley for garnish

Instructions:

1.Heat olive oil in a large skillet over medium heat. Season the chicken slices with salt, pepper, garlic powder, and Italian seasoning. Cook the chicken for 6-7 minutes until golden and cooked through. Remove and set aside.2.In the same skillet, melt the butter and add the heavy cream. Simmer for 3-4 minutes until slightly thickened.3.Stir in the grated Parmesan cheese until the sauce is smooth and creamy.4.Add the spiralized zucchini (zoodles) to the skillet, tossing them in the Alfredo sauce. Cook for 2-3 minutes until the zoodles are tender but still firm. 5.Return the cooked chicken to the skillet, tossing to coat in the sauce. Serve hot, garnished with fresh parsley if desired.

Chef's Tip: *For the best texture, lightly sauté the zoodles just before serving to avoid overcooking.*

Nutrition per Serving:

- **Calories:** 420
- **Protein:** 35g
- **Carbohydrates:** 5g
- **Fat:** 30g
- **Fiber:** 2g

4. Buffalo Chicken Lettuce Wraps

Servings: 4 • **Prep Time:** 10 minutes • **Cooking Time:** 15 minutes

Ingredients:

- 1 lb chicken breast, cooked and shredded
- 1/4 cup buffalo sauce (keto-friendly)
- 1 tbsp butter
- 1/4 cup ranch dressing (keto-friendly)
- 8 large romaine or iceberg lettuce leaves
- 1/4 cup shredded cheddar cheese
- 1/4 cup diced celery
- Optional: Blue cheese crumbles for garnish

Instructions:

1.In a skillet, melt the butter over medium heat. Add the shredded chicken and buffalo sauce, stirring to coat. Cook for 3-5 minutes until heated through.2.Lay out the lettuce leaves on a serving plate. Fill each leaf with a portion of the buffalo chicken mixture.3.Drizzle with ranch dressing and sprinkle with shredded cheddar cheese and diced celery. 4.Serve with blue cheese crumbles if desired.

Chef's Tip: *For a crispier texture, chill the lettuce leaves in the fridge before serving.*

Nutrition per Serving:

- **Calories:** 280
- **Protein:** 25g
- **Carbohydrates:** 3g
- **Fat:** 19g
- **Fiber:** 1g

5. Crispy Keto Chicken Tenders with Ranch

Servings: 4 • **Prep Time:** 10 minutes • **Cooking Time:** 20 minutes

Ingredients:
- 1 lb chicken tenders
- 1 cup pork rinds, crushed into crumbs
- 1/2 cup Parmesan cheese, grated
- 1 tsp garlic powder
- 1 tsp smoked paprika
- 1 large egg
- 1/4 cup almond flour
- 1/4 cup keto-friendly ranch dressing (for dipping)
- Salt and pepper to taste
- Olive oil spray for cooking

Instructions:
1.Preheat the oven to 400°F (200°C) and line a baking sheet with parchment paper.2.In a shallow bowl, mix the crushed pork rinds, Parmesan cheese, garlic powder, smoked paprika, salt, and pepper. 3.In a separate bowl, whisk the egg.4.Lightly coat the chicken tenders in almond flour, dip them in the egg, then press into the pork rind mixture to coat.5.Place the coated tenders on the prepared baking sheet and spray lightly with olive oil.6.Bake for 20 minutes, flipping halfway through, until golden brown and crispy.7.Serve with keto-friendly ranch dressing for dipping.

Chef's Tip: *For extra crispiness, broil the tenders for the last 2-3 minutes of baking.*

Nutrition per Serving:
- **Calories:** 350
- **Protein:** 30g
- **Carbohydrates:** 3g
- **Fat:** 23g
- **Fiber:** 1g

6. Keto Chicken Cordon Bleu

Servings: 4 • **Prep Time:** 15 minutes • **Cooking Time:** 30 minutes

Ingredients:
- 4 boneless, skinless chicken breasts
- 4 slices of ham (sugar-free)
- 4 slices of Swiss cheese
- 1/2 cup almond flour
- 1/2 cup grated Parmesan cheese
- 1 large egg
- 1/4 tsp garlic powder
- 1/4 tsp smoked paprika
- 2 tbsp butter
- Salt and pepper to taste

Instructions:
1.Preheat the oven to 375°F (190°C).2.Butterfly each chicken breast by cutting it horizontally, being careful not to slice all the way through. Open the breasts and lay a slice of ham and Swiss cheese inside each one. Fold the chicken breasts closed and secure with toothpicks if needed.3.In a shallow bowl, mix the almond flour, Parmesan cheese, garlic powder, paprika, salt, and pepper.4.In another bowl, whisk the egg. Dip each stuffed chicken breast in the egg and then coat with the almond flour mixture.5.In an ovenproof skillet, melt the butter over medium heat. Brown the chicken breasts for 2-3 minutes on each side until golden.6.Transfer the skillet to the preheated oven and bake for 25-30 minutes until the chicken is cooked through.7.Let the chicken rest for 5 minutes before serving.

Chef's Tip: *For a creamier finish, serve with a side of keto-friendly Dijon mustard sauce.*

Nutrition per Serving:
- **Calories:** 420
- **Protein:** 45g
- **Carbohydrates:** 4g
- **Fat:** 23g
- **Fiber:** 1g

7. Coconut Curry Chicken Thighs

Servings: 4 • **Prep Time:** 10 minutes • **Cooking Time:** 30 minutes

Ingredients:

- 4 bone-in chicken thighs, skin on
- 1 can (13.5 oz) full-fat coconut milk
- 2 tbsp red curry paste
- 1 tbsp olive oil
- 1 clove garlic, minced
- 1 tbsp fresh ginger, grated
- 1 tbsp lime juice
- 1 tsp ground turmeric
- 1/4 cup fresh cilantro for garnish
- Salt and pepper to taste

Instructions:

1. In a large skillet, heat olive oil over medium heat. Season the chicken thighs with salt and pepper, and sear them skin-side down for 6-7 minutes until crispy. Flip and cook for another 5 minutes. Remove from the skillet and set aside. 2. In the same skillet, sauté the garlic and ginger for 1 minute until fragrant. 3. Stir in the curry paste, coconut milk, turmeric, and lime juice. Bring to a simmer. 4. Return the chicken thighs to the skillet, skin-side up, and cover. Simmer on low heat for 20-25 minutes until the chicken is cooked through and the sauce has thickened. 5. Garnish with fresh cilantro before serving.

Chef's Tip: *Serve with cauliflower rice to soak up the flavorful coconut curry sauce.*

Nutrition per Serving:

- **Calories:** 420
- **Protein:** 25g
- **Carbohydrates:** 5g
- **Fat:** 34g
- **Fiber:** 1g

8. Keto Chicken Parmesan with Almond Flour

Servings: 4 • **Prep Time:** 10 minutes • **Cooking Time:** 25 minutes

Ingredients:

- 4 boneless, skinless chicken breasts
- 1 cup almond flour
- 1/2 cup grated Parmesan cheese
- 1 tsp garlic powder
- 1 tsp Italian seasoning
- 1 large egg
- 1/4 cup marinara sauce (sugar-free)
- 1/2 cup shredded mozzarella cheese
- 2 tbsp olive oil
- Salt and pepper to taste

Instructions:

1. Preheat the oven to 375°F (190°C). 2. In a shallow bowl, mix almond flour, Parmesan cheese, garlic powder, Italian seasoning, salt, and pepper. 3. In another bowl, whisk the egg. 4. Dip each chicken breast in the egg, then coat in the almond flour mixture. 5. Heat olive oil in a large ovenproof skillet over medium heat. Sear the coated chicken breasts for 3-4 minutes on each side until golden brown. 6. Spoon marinara sauce over each chicken breast, top with shredded mozzarella, and transfer the skillet to the preheated oven. Bake for 15 minutes or until the chicken is cooked through and the cheese is melted. 7. Serve hot with extra marinara sauce if desired.

Chef's Tip: *For an extra crispy crust, bake the chicken on a wire rack placed over the baking sheet to allow heat to circulate evenly.*

Nutrition per Serving:

- **Calories:** 450
- **Protein:** 42g
- **Carbohydrates:** 5g
- **Fat:** 28g
- **Fiber:** 2g

9.Creamy Bacon and Mushroom Chicken

<u>Servings:</u> 4 • <u>Prep Time:</u> 10 minutes • <u>Cooking Time:</u> 25 minutes

Ingredients:
- 4 boneless, skinless
- chicken breasts
- 6 slices of bacon, chopped
- 1 cup mushrooms, sliced
- 1/2 cup heavy cream
- 1/2 cup chicken broth
- 1/4 cup grated Parmesan cheese
- 2 cloves garlic, minced
- 1 tbsp butter
- Salt and pepper to taste
- Fresh parsley for garnish

Instructions:
1.In a large skillet, cook the bacon over medium heat until crispy. Remove and set aside, leaving the bacon fat in the pan.2.Season the chicken breasts with salt and pepper. In the same skillet, sear the chicken breasts for 4-5 minutes on each side until golden brown. Remove and set aside.3.Add the butter to the skillet and sauté the garlic and mushrooms for 3-4 minutes until softened.4.Stir in the chicken broth and heavy cream, scraping the bottom of the pan to release any browned bits.5.Return the chicken breasts to the skillet, add the Parmesan cheese, and simmer for 8-10 minutes until the chicken is cooked through and the sauce has thickened.6.Stir in the crispy bacon and garnish with fresh parsley before serving.

Chef's Tip: *For a richer sauce, add 2 tbsp cream cheese to the pan along with the heavy cream.*

Nutrition per Serving:
- **Calories:** 500
- **Protein:** 40g
- **Carbohydrates:** 4g
- **Fat:** 36g
- **Fiber:** 1g

10. Keto BBQ Grilled Chicken

<u>Servings:</u> 4 • <u>Prep Time:</u> 10 minutes (plus marinating time) • <u>Cooking Time:</u> 20 minutes

Ingredients:
- 4 bone-in chicken thighs, skin on
- 1/4 cup keto-friendly BBQ sauce
- 2 tbsp olive oil
- 1 tsp smoked paprika
- 1 tsp garlic powder
- 1/2 tsp salt
- 1/2 tsp black pepper
- Optional: Fresh cilantro for garnish

Instructions:
1.In a small bowl, mix olive oil, smoked paprika, garlic powder, salt, and pepper. Rub the mixture over the chicken thighs, then marinate for at least 30 minutes (or overnight for better flavor).2.Preheat the grill to medium heat.3.Grill the chicken thighs skin-side down for 7-8 minutes, then flip and cook for an additional 7-8 minutes.4.In the last 5 minutes of cooking, brush the chicken with the keto-friendly BBQ sauce, flipping as needed to avoid burning.5.Once the chicken reaches an internal temperature of 165°F (75°C), remove from the grill and let rest for 5 minutes before serving.6.Garnish with fresh cilantro if desired.

Chef's Tip: *For added smoky flavor, use wood chips in the grill or a cast-iron grill pan on the stove.*

Nutrition per Serving:
- **Calories:** 40
- **Protein:** 30g
- **Carbohydrates:** 4g
- **Fat:** 28g
- **Fiber:** 0g

CHAPTER 8

PORK RECIPES

1. Keto BBQ Pulled Pork

Servings: 6 • **Prep Time:** 10 minutes • **Cooking Time:** 6-8 hours (slow cooker)

Ingredients:

- 2 lbs pork shoulder (Boston butt)
- 1/2 cup keto-friendly BBQ sauce
- 1 tbsp smoked paprika
- 1 tbsp garlic powder
- 1 tsp cumin
- 1 tsp onion powder
- 1/2 tsp black pepper
- 1/2 tsp salt

Instructions:

1.In a small bowl, mix the smoked paprika, garlic powder, cumin, onion powder, salt, and pepper.2.Rub the spice mixture all over the pork shoulder.3.Place the pork in a slow cooker and cook on low for 6-8 hours, or until the pork is tender and easily shredded with a fork.4.Shred the pork using two forks, then stir in the keto BBQ sauce.5.Serve hot, optionally with a side of keto coleslaw.

Chef's Tip: *If you don't have a slow cooker, cook the pork in a Dutch oven at 300°F (150°C) for 3-4 hours..*

Nutrition per Serving:

- **Calories:** 370
- **Protein:** 36g
- **Carbohydrates:** 3g
- **Fat:** 24g
- **Fiber:** 1g

2. Keto Sausage and Cabbage Skillet

Servings: 4 • **Prep Time:** 10 minutes • **Cooking Time:** 20 minutes

Ingredients:

- 1 lb keto-friendly sausage (Italian or smoked), sliced
- 1/2 head green cabbage, thinly sliced
- 1/2 onion, diced
- 2 tbsp butter
- 1 tbsp olive oil
- 1/2 tsp garlic powder
- Salt and pepper to taste
- Optional: Fresh parsley for garnish

Instructions:

1.In a large skillet, heat olive oil over medium heat. Add the sausage slices and cook for 5-6 minutes until browned. Remove and set aside.
2.In the same skillet, melt the butter and add the diced onion. Cook for 2-3 minutes until softened.3. Add the sliced cabbage, garlic powder, salt, and pepper to the skillet. Cook for 8-10 minutes, stirring occasionally, until the cabbage is tender and slightly caramelized.4. Return the sausage to the skillet and cook for an additional 2-3 minutes to heat through.5.Garnish with fresh parsley if desired, and serve.

Chef's Tip: *For added flavor, deglaze the skillet with 1/4 cup of chicken broth or white wine after cooking the sausage.*

Nutrition per Serving:

- **Calories:** 370
- **Protein:** 18g
- **Carbohydrates:** 6g
- **Fat:** 30g
- **Fiber:** 2g

3. Keto Balsamic Glazed Pork Loin

Servings: 4 • Prep Time: 10 minutes • Cooking Time: 40 minutes

Ingredients:

* 1 pork loin (1.5 lbs)
* 1/4 cup balsamic vinegar (keto-friendly, with no added sugar)
* 2 tbsp olive oil
* 2 cloves garlic, minced
* 1 tsp fresh rosemary, chopped
* 1 tsp Dijon mustard
* Salt and pepper to taste

Instructions:

1.Preheat the oven to 375°F (190°C).2.In a small bowl, mix balsamic vinegar, olive oil, minced garlic, rosemary, Dijon mustard, salt, and pepper.3.Rub the balsamic mixture all over the pork loin and let it marinate for at least 30 minutes (optional for extra flavor).4.Place the pork loin on a baking sheet lined with parchment paper.5.Roast in the oven for 35-40 minutes or until the internal temperature reaches 145°F (63°C). Let the pork rest for 5 minutes before slicing.6. Drizzle the remaining pan juices over the sliced pork before serving.

Chef's Tip: *For a thicker glaze, reduce the balsamic mixture in a saucepan over medium heat until it thickens before pouring it over the*

Nutrition per Serving:

* **Calories:** 360
* **Protein:** 35g
* **Carbohydrates:** 3g
* **Fat:** 22g
* **Fiber:** 0g

4. Keto Pork Carnitas with Avocado Salsa

Servings: 6 • Prep Time: 10 minutes • Cooking Time: 6 hours (slow cooker)

Ingredients:

* 2 lbs pork shoulder (Boston butt), cubed
* 1 tbsp olive oil
* 1 tbsp cumin
* 1 tsp garlic powder
* 1 tsp smoked paprika
* 1 tsp chili powder
* 1/2 tsp salt
* 1/2 tsp black pepper
* Juice of 1 lime
* 1 avocado, diced
* 1/4 cup red onion, diced
* 2 tbsp fresh cilantro, chopped
* 1 tbsp lime juice for salsa
* Salt and pepper to taste for salsa

Instructions:

1.Rub the pork shoulder with cumin, garlic powder, smoked paprika, chili powder, salt, and pepper.2.Heat olive oil in a large skillet over medium heat and sear the pork cubes for 2-3 minutes on each side until browned. Transfer the pork to a slow cooker and add the juice of 1 lime. Cook on low for 6 hours or until the pork is tender and easy to shred.3.While the pork is cooking, make the avocado salsa by combining diced avocado, red onion, cilantro, lime juice, salt, and pepper.4.Once the pork is done, shred it with two forks and serve with the avocado salsa.

Chef's Tip: *For crispier carnitas, transfer the shredded pork to a baking sheet and broil for 3-4 minutes to crisp up the edges.*

Nutrition per Serving:

* **Calories:** 380
* **Protein:** 30g
* **Carbohydrates:** 4g
* **Fat:** 27g
* **Fiber:** 2g

5. Creamy Keto Tuscan Pork Chops

Servings: 4 • **Prep Time:** 10 minutes • **Cooking Time:** 20 minutes

Ingredients:
- 4 boneless pork chops
- 2 tbsp olive oil
- 2 tbsp butter
- 1 cup heavy cream
- 1/2 cup chicken broth
- 1/2 cup sun-dried tomatoes, chopped
- 3 cups fresh spinach
- 1/2 cup grated Parmesan cheese
- 2 cloves garlic, minced
- Salt and pepper to taste

Instructions:

1.Season the pork chops with salt and pepper. In a large skillet, heat olive oil over medium heat and sear the pork chops for 4-5 minutes per side until golden brown. Remove and set aside.2. In the same skillet, melt butter and sauté the minced garlic for 1 minute until fragrant.3.Stir in the chicken broth, heavy cream, and sun-dried tomatoes. Simmer for 5 minutes until the sauce thickens.4. Add the spinach and Parmesan cheese to the skillet, stirring until the spinach wilts and the sauce is creamy.5.Return the pork chops to the skillet, coating them with the sauce. Simmer for 3-4 minutes to heat through.

Chef's Tip: *Add a pinch of red pepper flakes to the sauce for a spicy kick.*

Nutrition per Serving:
- **Calories:** 480
- **Protein:** 35g
- **Carbohydrates:** 5g
- **Fat:** 36g
- **Fiber:** 1g

6. Keto Pork Rind-Crusted Pork Chops

Servings: 4 • **Prep Time:** 10 minutes • **Cooking Time:** 15 minutes

Ingredients:
- 4 boneless pork chops
- 1 cup pork rinds, crushed into fine crumbs
- 1/2 cup Parmesan cheese, grated
- 1 large egg
- 1 tbsp Dijon mustard
- 1/4 tsp garlic powder
- 1/4 tsp paprika
- 2 tbsp olive oil for frying
- Salt and pepper to taste

Instructions:

1.In a shallow bowl, mix the crushed pork rinds, Parmesan cheese, garlic powder, paprika, salt, and pepper.2.In another bowl, whisk the egg with Dijon mustard.3.Dip each pork chop in the egg mixture, then coat with the pork rind mixture, pressing firmly to adhere.4.Heat olive oil in a large skillet over medium heat. Fry the pork chops for 5-6 minutes per side until golden and cooked through.5.Remove from the skillet and let rest for a few minutes before serving.

Chef's Tip: *For extra crispiness, finish the pork chops in the oven at 350°F (175°C) for 5 minutes after frying.*

Nutrition per Serving:
- **Calories:** 450
- **Protein:** 35g
- **Carbohydrates:** 2g
- **Fat:** 33g
- **Fiber:** 0g

7. Slow-Cooked Keto Pork Ribs

Servings: 6 • **Prep Time:** 10 minutes • **Cooking Time:** 6-8 hours (slow cooker)

Ingredients:

- 3 lbs pork baby back ribs
- 1 tbsp smoked paprika
- 1 tbsp garlic powder
- 1 tsp onion powder
- 1 tsp ground cumin
- 1 tsp salt
- 1/2 tsp black pepper
- 1/2 cup keto-friendly BBQ sauce

Instructions:

1.In a small bowl, combine the smoked paprika, garlic powder, onion powder, cumin, salt, and pepper.2.Rub the spice mixture evenly over the pork ribs.3.Place the ribs in a slow cooker, cover, and cook on low for 6-8 hours until the ribs are tender and easily pulled apart with a fork.4.Remove the ribs from the slow cooker and brush them with keto-friendly BBQ sauce.5.For extra caramelization, broil the ribs in the oven for 3-5 minutes until the sauce is bubbly and slightly charred.6.Let the ribs rest for a few minutes before serving.

Chef's Tip: *For added flavor, marinate the ribs in the spice rub overnight before cooking.*

Nutrition per Serving:

- **Calories:** 450
- **Protein:** 35g
- **Carbohydrates:** 3g
- **Fat:** 33g
- **Fiber:** 1g

8. Keto Pork and Mushroom Casserole

Servings: 4 • **Prep Time:** 10 minutes • **Cooking Time:** 35 minutes

Ingredients:

- 1 lb pork loin, thinly sliced
- 2 cups mushrooms, sliced
- 1/2 cup heavy cream
- 1/2 cup shredded
- mozzarella cheese
- 1/4 cup Parmesan cheese, grated
- 2 tbsp butter
- 1 tsp garlic powder
- 1/2 tsp onion powder
- Salt and pepper to taste
- 1 tbsp fresh parsley for garnish

Instructions:

1.Preheat the oven to 375°F (190°C).2. In a skillet, melt the butter over medium heat. Add the sliced pork and cook for 5-6 minutes until browned. Remove and set aside.3. In the same skillet, sauté the mushrooms for 3-4 minutes until softened.4.Stir in the garlic powder, onion powder, heavy cream, and Parmesan cheese. Simmer for 2-3 minutes until the sauce thickens slightly.5. Return the pork to the skillet and mix everything together. Transfer to a baking dish, top with mozzarella cheese, and bake for 20 minutes until bubbly and golden.6. Garnish with fresh parsley before serving.

Chef's Tip: *For added flavor, sprinkle some crushed pork rinds over the top before baking for a crunchy crust.*

Nutrition per Serving:

- **Calories:** 430
- **Protein:** 33g
- **Carbohydrates:** 4g
- **Fat:** 32g
- **Fiber:** 1g

9. Keto Sausage-Stuffed Bell Peppers

Servings: 4 • **Prep Time:** 10 minutes • **Cooking Time:** 30 minutes

Ingredients:

- 4 large bell peppers, tops cut off and seeds removed
- 1 lb ground sausage (sugar-free)
- 1/2 cup shredded mozzarella cheese
- 1/2 cup ricotta cheese
- 1/4 cup Parmesan cheese, grated
- 1 tsp garlic powder
- 1/2 tsp Italian seasoning
- Salt and pepper to taste

Instructions:

1.Preheat the oven to 375°F (190°C).2. In a skillet, cook the sausage over medium heat for 6-7 minutes until browned. Drain excess fat if needed. 3.In a bowl, combine the cooked sausage, ricotta cheese, mozzarella cheese, Parmesan cheese, garlic powder, Italian seasoning, salt, and pepper.4.Stuff the bell peppers with the sausage mixture and place them in a baking dish.5.Bake for 25-30 minutes, or until the peppers are tender and the filling is golden and bubbly.6.Let the peppers cool for a few minutes before serving.

Chef'sTip: *For extra flavor, top the stuffed peppers with additional shredded mozzarella and broil for the last 2-3 minutes of baking.*

Nutrition per Serving:

- **Calories:** 420
- **Protein:** 30g
- **Carbohydrates:** 6g
- **Fat:** 30g
- **Fiber:** 2g

10. Keto Ham and Cheese Roll-Ups

Servings: 4 • **Prep Time:** 5 minutes

Ingredients:

- 8 slices deli ham (sugar-free)
- 4 slices Swiss cheese
- 2 tbsp cream cheese, softened
- 1 tsp Dijon mustard
- 1/4 tsp garlic powder
- 1/4 tsp paprika
- Fresh parsley for garnish (optional)

Instructions:

1.In a small bowl, mix the cream cheese, Dijon mustard, garlic powder, and paprika.2.Lay a slice of ham flat and spread a thin layer of the cream cheese mixture on top.3.Place a slice of Swiss cheese on the ham, then roll up tightly.4.Repeat with the remaining ham, cream cheese mixture, and Swiss cheese.5.Slice each roll into bite-sized pieces if desired, or serve as whole roll-ups.6.Garnish with fresh parsley before serving.

Chef's Tip: *For an added crunch, lightly toast the roll-ups in a skillet over medium heat for 1-2 minutes per side.*

Nutrition per Serving:

- **Calories:** 240
- **Protein:** 20g
- **Carbohydrates:** 2g
- **Fat:** 18g
- **Fiber:** 0g

CHAPTER 9

BEEF &LAMB

RECIPES

1. Keto Butter Garlic Steak Bites

<u>Servings:</u> 4 • <u>**Prep Time:**</u> 10 minutes • <u>**Cooking Time:**</u> 10 minutes

Ingredients:
- 1.5 lbs sirloin steak, cut into bite-sized pieces
- 3 tbsp butter, divided
- 4 cloves garlic, minced
- 1 tbsp olive oil
- Salt and pepper to taste
- 1 tbsp fresh parsley, chopped (optional)
-

Instructions:

1.Season the steak bites with salt and pepper.2. Heat olive oil in a large skillet over medium-high heat. Add 1 tbsp of butter.3. Once the butter is melted, add the steak bites to the skillet in a single layer. Sear the steak for 2-3 minutes per side until browned and cooked to your desired doneness. Remove from the skillet and set aside.4. In the same skillet, add the remaining 2 tbsp of butter and the minced garlic. Sauté for 1 minute until fragrant.5. Return the steak bites to the skillet and toss them in the garlic butter for 1-2 minutes.6. Garnish with fresh parsley and serve.

Chef's Tip: *For added flavor, use a mix of olive oil and ghee for searing the steak.*

Nutrition per Serving:
- **Calories:** 380
- **Protein:** 30g
- **Carbohydrates:** 1g
- **Fat:** 29g
- **Fiber:** 0g

2. Keto Beef Stroganoff with Zoodles

<u>Servings:</u> 4 • <u>**Prep Time:**</u> 10 minutes • <u>**Cooking Time:**</u> 25 minutes

Ingredients:
- 1 lb ground beef
- 1/2 cup beef broth
- 1/2 cup heavy cream
- 1/2 cup sour cream
- 1 small onion, diced
- 2 cloves garlic, minced
- 1 tsp smoked paprika
- 2 tbsp butter
- 3 medium zucchini, spiralized into zoodles
- Salt and pepper to taste
- 1 tbsp fresh parsley for garnish

Instructions:

1.Heat 1 tbsp of butter in a skillet over medium heat. Add the onion and garlic, sautéing for 2-3 minutes until soft.2. Add the ground beef to the skillet, breaking it apart and cooking until browned, about 5-6 minutes. Drain any excess fat.3. Stir in the beef broth, heavy cream, sour cream, smoked paprika, salt, and pepper. Simmer for 10 minutes until the sauce thickens.4. While the beef is simmering, heat the remaining 1 tbsp of butter in a separate skillet and sauté the zoodles for 2-3 minutes until slightly softened.5. Serve the beef stroganoff over the zoodles and garnish with fresh parsley.

Chef's Tip: *For a richer flavor, use full-fat sour cream and cook the zoodles until just tender to avoid sogginess.*

Nutrition per Serving:
- **Calories:** 420
- **Protein:** 25g
- **Carbohydrates:** 6g
- **Fat:** 34g
- **Fiber:** 2g

3. Grilled Keto Lamb Chops with Herb Butter

Servings: 4 • **Prep Time:** 10 minutes • **Cooking Time:** 10 minutes

Ingredients:

- 8 lamb chops (about 1-inch thick)
- 2 tbsp olive oil
- 1 tsp garlic powder
- 1 tsp dried rosemary
- 1/2 tsp salt
- 1/2 tsp black pepper
- 4 tbsp butter, softened
- 1 tbsp fresh parsley, chopped
- 1 tsp lemon zest

Instructions

1.Preheat the grill to medium-high heat.2.Rub the lamb chops with olive oil, garlic powder, rosemary, salt, and pepper.3.Grill the lamb chops for 4-5 minutes per side, depending on your desired level of doneness.4.While the lamb chops are grilling, mix the softened butter, parsley, and lemon zest in a small bowl.5.Remove the lamb chops from the grill and immediately top each one with a dollop of herb butter.6.Let the lamb chops rest for 5 minutes before serving.

Chef's Tip: *Let the lamb chops come to room temperature before grilling for more even cooking.*

Nutrition per Serving:

- **Calories:** 420
- **Protein:** 28g
- **Carbohydrates:** 1g
- **Fat:** 34g
- **Fiber:** 0g

4. Keto Meatballs in Tomato Basil Sauce

Servings: 4 • **Prep Time:** 15 minutes • **Cooking Time:** 25 minutes

Ingredients:

For the meatballs:
- 1 lb ground beef
- 1/2 cup Parmesan cheese, grated
- 1 egg
- 1 tsp garlic powder
- 1 tsp Italian seasoning
- Salt and pepper to taste

For the sauce:
- 1 cup keto-friendly tomato sauce (no added sugar)
- 1/4 cup fresh basil, chopped
- 2 cloves garlic, minced
- 1 tbsp olive oil
- Salt and pepper to taste

Instructions:

1.Preheat the oven to 375°F (190°C).2. In a large bowl, mix the ground beef, Parmesan cheese, egg, garlic powder, Italian seasoning, salt, and pepper. Form the mixture into 12 meatballs.3. Place the meatballs on a baking sheet and bake for 20 minutes, or until cooked through.4.While the meatballs are baking, heat olive oil in a saucepan over medium heat. Add the minced garlic and sauté for 1 minute.5. Stir in the tomato sauce, fresh basil, salt, and pepper. Simmer for 10 minutes until slightly thickened. 6.Once the meatballs are cooked, add them to the sauce and simmer for another 5 minutes.7. Serve the meatballs with extra fresh basil for garnish.

Chef's Tip: *Serve over zucchini noodles or spaghetti squash for a low-carb "pasta" option.*

Nutrition per Serving:

- **Calories:** 380
- **Protein:** 28g
- **Carbohydrates:** 4g
- **Fat:** 28g
- **Fiber:** 1g

5. Spicy Keto Beef Tacos in Lettuce Wraps

Servings: 4 • **Prep Time:** 10 minutes • **Cooking Time:** 15 minutes

Ingredients:
- 1 lb ground beef (80/20)
- 1 tbsp olive oil
- 1 tbsp taco seasoning
- (keto-friendly)
- 1/2 cup shredded cheddar cheese
- 1/2 cup sour cream
- 1 avocado, sliced
- 8 large lettuce leaves (romaine or iceberg)
- 1/4 cup salsa (sugar-free)
- 1/4 cup diced red onion
- Salt and pepper to taste

Instructions:

1.Heat olive oil in a skillet over medium heat. Add the ground beef and cook for 8-10 minutes, breaking it apart until browned and cooked through.2. Drain any excess fat and add the taco seasoning, stirring to combine. Cook for another 2-3 minutes.3. Lay the lettuce leaves out on a platter and spoon the beef mixture into each leaf.4.Top each taco with shredded cheddar cheese, sour cream, avocado slices, salsa, and diced red onion.5.Serve immediately.

Nutrition per Serving:
- **Calories:** 420
- **Protein:** 25g
- **Carbohydrates:** 6g
- **Fat:** 32g
- **Fiber:** 4g

Chef's Tip: *For extra spice, add chopped jalapeños or a sprinkle of chili flakes.*

6. Keto Beef Brisket with Garlic Butter

Servings: 6 • **Prep Time:** 10 minutes • **Cooking Time:** 3-4 hours (oven) or 8 hours (slow cooker)

Ingredients:
- 3 lbs beef brisket
- 4 cloves garlic, minced
- 1/4 cup butter, melted
- 1 tbsp olive oil
- 1 tsp smoked paprika
- 1 tsp garlic powder
- 1/2 tsp onion powder
- Salt and pepper to taste
- 1 cup beef broth

Instructions:

1.Preheat the oven to 300°F (150°C) or set your slow cooker to low.2.In a small bowl, combine melted butter, minced garlic, smoked paprika, garlic powder, onion powder, salt, and pepper.3.Rub the spice mixture all over the brisket.4.Heat olive oil in a large ovenproof skillet over medium-high heat. Sear the brisket for 3-4 minutes on each side until browned.5.Add beef broth to the skillet, cover with foil or a lid, and transfer to the oven. Cook for 3-4 hours, or until the brisket is tender and easily pulled apart with a fork.6. For the slow cooker, place the seared brisket in the cooker, add broth, and cook on low for 8 hours.7.Let the brisket rest for 10 minutes before slicing and serving.

Nutrition per Serving:
- **Calories:** 480
- **Protein:** 35g
- **Carbohydrates:** 3g
- **Fat:** 36g
- **Fiber:** 0g

Chef's Tip: *For an extra garlic flavor, drizzle the brisket with garlic butter sauce right before serving.*

7. Keto Lamb Curry with Coconut Milk

Servings: 4 • **Prep Time:** 10 minutes • **Cooking Time:** 45 minutes

Ingredients:

- 1.5 lbs lamb stew meat, cubed
- 1 can (13.5 oz) full-fat coconut milk
- 2 tbsp coconut oil
- 1 onion, diced
- 2 cloves garlic, minced
- 1 tbsp ginger, minced
- 1 tbsp curry powder
- 1 tsp ground cumin
- 1 tsp turmeric
- 1/2 tsp chili flakes (optional)
- Salt and pepper to taste
- 1/4 cup fresh cilantro for garnish

Instructions:

1.Heat coconut oil in a large pot over medium heat. Add the diced onion and sauté for 3-4 minutes until softened.2. Stir in the garlic, ginger, curry powder, cumin, turmeric, and chili flakes (if using). Cook for 1-2 minutes until fragrant.3. Add the lamb to the pot and brown on all sides, about 5-6 minutes.4.Pour in the coconut milk, reduce the heat, and simmer for 35-40 minutes until the lamb is tender and the sauce has thickened.5.Season with salt and pepper to taste. Garnish with fresh cilantro before serving.

Chef's Tip: *For a thicker sauce, simmer uncovered for the last 10 minutes*

Nutrition per Serving:

- **Calories:** 550
- **Protein:** 30g
- **Carbohydrates:** 6g
- **Fat:** 45g
- **Fiber:** 2g

8. Keto Philly Cheesesteak Skillet

Servings: 4 • **Prep Time:** 10 minutes • **Cooking Time:** 15 minutes

Ingredients:

- 1 lb thinly sliced steak (ribeye or sirloin)
- 1 green bell pepper, sliced
- 1 onion, sliced
- 1/2 cup mushrooms, sliced
- 1 tbsp olive oil
- 2 tbsp butter
- 1/2 tsp garlic powder
- 1/2 cup provolone cheese, shredded
- 1/2 cup mozzarella cheese, shredded
- Salt and pepper to taste

Instructions:

1.Heat olive oil in a large skillet over medium-high heat. Add the sliced steak and cook for 3-4 minutes until browned. Remove from the skillet and set aside.2. In the same skillet, melt butter and sauté the onions, bell pepper, and mushrooms for 5-6 minutes until softened.3. Add the steak back to the skillet and season with garlic powder, salt, and pepper. 4.Sprinkle provolone and mozzarella cheese over the steak and veggies. Cover the skillet and cook for 2-3 minutes until the cheese is melted and bubbly.5. Serve hot.

Chef's Tip: *For added flavor, add a dash of Worcestershire sauce or hot sauce to the skillet before adding the cheese.*

Nutrition per Serving:

- **Calories:** 480
- **Protein:** 32g
- **Carbohydrates:** 6g
- **Fat:** 36g
- **Fiber:** 2g

9. Keto Beef and Bacon Burgers

Servings: 4 • **Prep Time:** 10 minutes • **Cooking Time:** 10 minutes

Ingredients:

- 1 lb ground beef (80/20)
- 4 slices bacon, chopped
- 1/4 cup shredded cheddar cheese
- 1 tbsp Dijon mustard
- 1/2 tsp garlic powder
- Salt and pepper to taste
- 4 large lettuce leaves (for serving)

Instructions:

1.In a skillet, cook the chopped bacon until crispy. Drain on paper towels and set aside.2.In a large bowl, combine the ground beef, shredded cheddar, cooked bacon, Dijon mustard, garlic powder, salt, and pepper. 3.Form the mixture into 4 burger patties.4.Heat a grill or skillet over medium-high heat and cook the burgers for 4-5 minutes per side, or until cooked to your desired doneness.5.Serve the burgers in large lettuce leaves, topped with your favorite keto-friendly toppings (e.g., avocado, mayonnaise, pickles).

Chef's Tip: *For added flavor, mix 1 tbsp of Worcestershire sauce into the burger mixture before cooking.*

Nutrition per Serving:

- **Calories:** 450
- **Protein:** 28g
- **Carbohydrates:** 2g
- **Fat:** 35g
- **Fiber:** 0g

10. Rosemary Garlic Grilled Lamb Racks

Servings: 4 • **Prep Time:** 10 minutes • **Cooking Time:** 20 minutes

Ingredients:

- 2 racks of lamb (about 1.5 lbs)
- 2 tbsp olive oil
- 2 tbsp fresh rosemary, chopped
- 4 cloves garlic, minced
- 1 tsp lemon zest
- Salt and pepper to taste

Instructions:

1.Preheat the grill to medium-high heat.2.In a small bowl, mix olive oil, chopped rosemary, minced garlic, lemon zest, salt, and pepper.3.Rub the herb mixture all over the lamb racks.4.Grill the lamb racks for 10-12 minutes per side, depending on your desired level of doneness (130°F for medium-rare).5.Remove from the grill and let the lamb rest for 5 minutes before slicing and serving.

Chef's Tip: *For extra flavor, marinate the lamb in the herb mixture for at least 1 hour before grilling.*

Nutrition per Serving:

- **Calories:** 480
- **Protein:** 35g
- **Carbohydrates:** 1g
- **Fat:** 37g
- **Fiber:** 0g

CHAPTER 10
FISH & SEAFOOD RECIPES

1. Crispy Keto Fish Tacos in Cabbage Wraps

Servings: 4 • **Prep Time:** 10 minutes • **Cooking Time:** 15 minutes

Ingredients:

- 1 lb white fish (cod, tilapia, or halibut), cut into strips
- 1/2 cup almond flour
- 1/4 cup grated Parmesan cheese
- 1 tsp garlic powder
- 1 tsp paprika
- 1 large egg, beaten
- 2 tbsp olive oil
- 8 large cabbage leaves (for wraps)
- 1/2 cup sour cream
- 1 tbsp lime juice
- 1/4 cup fresh cilantro, chopped
- Salt and pepper to taste

Instructions:

1.In a shallow bowl, mix the almond flour, Parmesan cheese, garlic powder, paprika, salt, and pepper.2. Dip the fish strips in the beaten egg, then coat them in the almond flour mixture.3. Heat olive oil in a skillet over medium heat. Fry the fish strips for 3-4 minutes on each side until golden and crispy.4. In a small bowl, mix the sour cream, lime juice, and cilantro. Set aside.5. To assemble the tacos, place the crispy fish strips in cabbage leaves and top with a dollop of the lime cilantro sour cream. 6.Serve with extra lime wedges.

Chef's Tip: *For added crunch, serve the fish tacos with sliced radishes or avocado slices.*

Nutrition per Serving:

- **Calories:** 380
- **Protein:** 28g
- **Carbohydrates:** 5g
- **Fat:** 28g
- **Fiber:** 3g

2. Keto Lobster Bisque

Servings: 4 • **Prep Time:** 10 minutes • **Cooking Time:** 20 minutes

Ingredients:

- 1 lb lobster meat (pre-cooked, chopped)
- 2 tbsp butter
- 1 small onion, finely diced
- 2 cloves garlic, minced
- 1/2 cup heavy cream
- 1/4 cup dry white wine (optional)
- 2 cups seafood or chicken broth
- 1 tsp paprika
- 1/4 tsp cayenne pepper (optional)
- Salt and pepper to taste
- Fresh parsley for garnish

Instructions:

1.In a large pot, melt the butter over medium heat. Add the onion and garlic, sautéing for 3-4 minutes until softened.2. Stir in the paprika and cayenne pepper, and cook for another 1 minute.3.Add the broth and white wine (if using), and bring to a simmer. Let it cook for 5 minutes to allow the flavors to meld.4. Stir in the heavy cream and lobster meat, and simmer for another 5 minutes.5.Season with salt and pepper to taste, and serve garnished with fresh parsley.

Chef's Tip: *For a smoother bisque, blend the soup with an immersion blender before adding the lobster meat.*

Nutrition per Serving:

- **Calories:** 420
- **Protein:** 30g
- **Carbohydrates:** 5g
- **Fat:** 30g
- **Fiber:** 1g

3. Grilled Keto Swordfish with Olive

Servings: 4 • **Prep Time:** 10 minutes • **Cooking Time:** 10 minutes

Ingredients:

For the Swordfish:
- 4 swordfish steaks (about 6 oz each)
- 2 tbsp olive oil
- 1 clove garlic, minced
- 1 tsp lemon zest
- Salt and pepper to taste

For the Olive Tapenade:
- 1/2 cup pitted black olives, chopped
- 1/4 cup green olives, chopped
- 2 tbsp capers, drained
- 2 tbsp olive oil
- 1 tbsp lemon juice
- 1 tbsp fresh parsley, chopped
- Salt and pepper to taste

Instructions:

1.Preheat the grill to medium-high heat.2. Brush the swordfish steaks with olive oil, and season with garlic, lemon zest, salt, and pepper.3.Grill the swordfish for 4-5 minutes per side, until cooked through and opaque. 4.While the swordfish is grilling, mix the chopped black and green olives, capers, olive oil, lemon juice, parsley, salt, and pepper in a small bowl to make the tapenade.5. Serve the grilled swordfish topped with the olive tapenade.

Chef's Tip: *For a smoky flavor, grill the swordfish over wood chips or a charcoal grill.*

Nutrition per Serving:
- **Calories:** 430
- **Protein:** 35g
- **Carbohydrates:** 3g
- **Fat:** 32g
- **Fiber:** 1g

4. Keto Cajun Shrimp Skillet

Servings: 4 • **Prep Time:** 10 minutes • **Cooking Time:** 10 minutes

Ingredients:
- 1 lb large shrimp, peeled and deveined
- 2 tbsp olive oil
- 1 tbsp Cajun seasoning
- 2 cloves garlic, minced
- 1/2 red bell pepper, sliced
- 1/2 green bell pepper, sliced
- 1/2 small onion, sliced
- 1 tbsp butter
- Fresh parsley for garnish
- Salt and pepper to taste

Instructions:

1.Heat 1 tbsp of olive oil in a large skillet over medium heat. Add the shrimp, season with Cajun seasoning, and cook for 2-3 minutes per side until pink. Remove the shrimp from the skillet and set aside.2. In the same skillet, heat the remaining olive oil and butter. Add the sliced bell peppers, onion, and minced garlic. Sauté for 3-4 minutes until tender.3. Return the shrimp to the skillet and toss everything together. Cook for another 1-2 minutes to heat through.4. Garnish with fresh parsley and serve hot.

Chef's Tip: *Add a squeeze of fresh lemon juice to brighten up the flavors.*

Nutrition per Serving:
- **Calories:** 310
- **Protein:** 25g
- **Carbohydrates:** 5g
- **Fat:** 21g
- **Fiber:** 2g

5. Keto Crab Cakes with Spicy Mayo

<u>Servings:</u> 4 • <u>Prep Time:</u> 15 minutes • <u>Cooking Time:</u> 10 minutes

Ingredients:
Ingredients for Crab Cakes:
- 1 lb lump crab meat
- 1/4 cup almond flour
- 1 large egg
- 1 tbsp Dijon mustard
- 1 tbsp mayonnaise (keto-friendly)
- 1 tbsp fresh parsley, chopped
- 1/2 tsp Old Bay seasoning
- 1/2 tsp garlic powder
- 2 tbsp butter (for frying)
- Salt and pepper to taste

Ingredients for Spicy Mayo:
- 1/4 cup mayonnaise (keto-friendly)
- 1 tsp hot sauce (adjust to taste)
- 1 tsp lime juice

Instructions:

1.In a large bowl, mix together the crab meat, almond flour, egg, Dijon mustard, mayonnaise, parsley, Old Bay seasoning, garlic powder, salt, and pepper.2.Form the mixture into 8 small patties.3.Heat the butter in a skillet over medium heat. Fry the crab cakes for 3-4 minutes per side, until golden brown and crispy.4.In a small bowl, mix the spicy mayo ingredients together.5.Serve the crab cakes with a drizzle of spicy mayo on top.

Chef's Tip: *To prevent the crab cakes from falling apart, chill them in the refrigerator for 30 minutes before frying.*

Nutrition per Serving:
- **Calories:** 380
- **Protein:** 25g
- **Carbohydrates:** 3g
- **Fat:** 29g
- **Fiber:** 1g

6. Keto Shrimp Alfredo over Zucchini Noodles

<u>Servings:</u> 4 • <u>Prep Time:</u> 10 minutes • <u>Cooking Time:</u> 15 minutes

Ingredients:
- 1 lb large shrimp, peeled and deveined
- 4 medium zucchini, spiralized into zoodles
- 2 tbsp butter
- 2 tbsp olive oil
- 1/2 cup heavy cream
- 1/4 cup Parmesan cheese, grated
- 2 cloves garlic, minced
- 1 tsp garlic powder
- Salt and pepper to taste
- Fresh parsley for garnish

Instructions:

1.In a large skillet, heat the olive oil and butter over medium heat. Add the shrimp, garlic, salt, and pepper, and cook for 2-3 minutes per side until pink and cooked through. Remove the shrimp from the skillet and set aside.2.In the same skillet, add the heavy cream, Parmesan cheese, garlic powder, salt, and pepper. Stir and simmer for 3-4 minutes until the sauce thickens.3.Add the zucchini noodles to the skillet and toss them in the Alfredo sauce for 2-3 minutes until just tender.4.Return the cooked shrimp to the skillet and toss to combine. Garnish with fresh parsley before serving.

Chef's Tip: *For extra creaminess, stir in 2 oz of cream cheese while simmering the Alfredo sauce.*

Nutrition per Serving:
- **Calories:** 380
- **Protein:** 26g
- **Carbohydrates:** 6g
- **Fat:** 28g
- **Fiber:** 2g

7. Baked Parmesan Crusted

Servings: 4 • **Prep Time:** 10 minutes • **Cooking Time:** 15 minutes

Ingredients:

- 4 (6 oz/170g each)
- tilapia fillets
- 1/2 cup (50g) grated
- Parmesan cheese
- 1/4 cup (30g) almond flour
- 2 tbsp (30ml) melted butter
- 1/2 tsp (2g) dried basil

- 1/2 tsp (2g) dried oregano
- 1/2 tsp (2g) garlic powder
- 1/4 tsp (1g) salt
- 1/4 tsp (1g) black pepper
- Lemon wedges, for garnish

Instructions:

1.Preheat Oven: Preheat oven to 400°F (200°C). Line a baking sheet with parchment paper.2.Prepare Coating: In a bowl, mix Parmesan cheese, almond flour, dried basil, oregano, garlic powder, salt, and pepper.3.Coat Fish: Dip each tilapia fillet in melted butter, then coat with the Parmesan mixture. Place on the prepared baking sheet.4.Bake: Bake for 12-15 minutes, or until tilapia is opaque and flakes easily with a fork.5.Serve: Garnish with lemon wedges and serve.

Chef's Tip: *For an extra golden and crispy finish, switch to broil for the last 2 minutes of baking. This will give the Parmesan crust a perfect crunchy texture without overcooking the fish. Keep a close eye on it to prevent burning.*

Nutrition per Serving:

- **Calories:** 320
- **Protein:** 35g
- **Carbohydrates:** 4g
- **Fat:** 19g
- **Fiber:** 1g

8. Spicy Garlic Butter Scallops

Servings: 4 • **Prep Time:** 10 minutes • **Cooking Time:** 10 minutes

Ingredients:

- 1 lb (450g) large sea scallops
- 3 tbsp (45g) unsalted butter
- 3 cloves garlic, minced
- 1/2 tsp (2g) red pepper flakes
- 1/2 tsp (2g) paprika
- 1/2 tsp (2g) salt
- 1/4 tsp (1g) black pepper
- Fresh parsley, chopped (for garnish)

Instructions:

1.Prepare Scallops: Pat scallops dry with paper towels and season with salt, pepper, and paprika.2. Cook Garlic: In a large skillet, melt butter over medium heat. Add minced garlic and red pepper flakes; cook for 1 minute. 3.Sear Scallops: Add scallops to the skillet and cook for 2-3 minutes per side, until golden brown and opaque.4. Serve: Garnish with chopped parsley and serve immediately.

Chef's Tip: *For an even deeper flavor and crispier texture, make sure the skillet is very hot before adding the scallops. This will create a beautiful golden sear without overcooking the scallops, locking in the juices while ensuring a caramelized crust. Avoid overcrowding the pan to achieve the best sear.*

Nutrition per Serving:

- **Calories:** 270
- **Protein:** 22g
- **Carbohydrates:** 3g
- **Fat:** 18g
- **Fiber:** 0g

9. Keto Stuffed Salmon with Cream Cheese

Servings: 4 • **Prep Time:** 15 minutes • **Cooking Time:** 20 minutes

Ingredients:

- 4 (6 oz/170g each) salmon fillets
- 4 oz (115g) cream cheese, softened
- 1/4 cup (30g) grated Parmesancheese
- 2 tbsp (30g) chopped fresh dill
- 2 tbsp (30g) chopped fresh chives
- 1 clove garlic, minced
- 1/2 tsp (2g) salt
- 1/4 tsp (1g) black pepper
- 1 tbsp (15ml) olive oil

Instructions:

1.Prepare Filling: In a bowl, mix cream cheese, Parmesan cheese, dill, chives, garlic, salt, and pepper.2. Stuff Salmon: Cut a slit in the side of each salmon fillet to create a pocket. Fill each pocket with the cream cheese mixture.3. Preheat Oven: Preheat oven to 375°F (190°C).4. Bake Salmon: Place stuffed salmon fillets on a baking sheet and brush with olive oil. Bake for 15-20 minutes, or until salmon is cooked through. 5.Serve: Serve warm.

Chef's Tip: *For added flavor and a crispy finish, sear the salmon fillets in a hot skillet with olive oil for 2-3 minutes per side before transferring them to the oven. This will give the salmon a beautiful golden crust while keeping the inside tender and juicy.*

Nutrition per Serving:

- **Calories:** 350
- **Protein**: 30g
- **Carbohydrates**: 4g
- **Fat:** 23g
- **Fiber:** 1g

10. Keto Tuna-Stuffed Avocados

Servings: 4 • **Prep Time:** 10 minutes • **Cooking Time:** 0 minutes

Ingredients:

- 2 ripe avocados
- 1 can (5 oz/140g) tuna in olive oil, drained
- 1/4 cup (60g) mayonnaise
- 1 tbsp (15g) lemon juice
- 1 tbsp (15g) chopped fresh chives
- 1/2 tsp (2g) dried dill
- Salt and pepper, to taste

Instructions:

1.Prepare Avocados: Cut avocados in half and remove the pit. Scoop out a little bit of the flesh to make more room for the tuna.2.Mix Tuna Filling: In a bowl, combine tuna, mayonnaise, lemon juice, chives, dill, salt, and pepper.3.Stuff Avocados: Spoon the tuna mixture into the avocado halves.4.Serve: Garnish with extra chives, if desired. Serve immediately.

Chef's Tip: *For an added crunch and texture contrast, sprinkle chopped toasted nuts (such as almonds or walnuts) or crispy bacon bits on top of the stuffed avocados before serving. This will elevate the dish with extra flavor and texture while keeping it keto-friendly.*

Nutrition per Serving:

- **Calories:** 320
- **Protein:** 18g
- **Carbohydrates:** 8g
- **Fat:** 25g
- **Fiber:** 6g

CHAPTER 11
VEGETARIAN RECIPES

1. Keto Cauliflower Mac and Cheese

Servings: 4 • **Prep Time:** 10 minutes • **Cooking Time:** 15 minutes

Ingredients:
- 1 large head of cauliflower, cut into florets
- 1 cup heavy cream
- 1 1/2 cups shredded cheddar cheese
- 1/2 cup cream cheese
- 1/4 cup grated Parmesan cheese
- 1/2 tsp garlic powder
- 1/2 tsp mustard powder
- Salt and pepper to taste
- 1/4 tsp paprika (for garnish)

Instructions:

1.Steam or boil the cauliflower florets for 5-7 minutes until tender. Drain and set aside.2. In a saucepan over medium heat, combine the heavy cream and cream cheese. Stir until the cream cheese melts and the mixture is smooth.3. Add the cheddar cheese, Parmesan cheese, garlic powder, mustard powder, salt, and pepper. Stir until the cheese sauce is fully melted and smooth.4. Toss the cooked cauliflower in the cheese sauce until well-coated.5.Transfer to a serving dish and garnish with paprika..

Chef's Tip: *For a crispy top, transfer the mac and cheese to an oven-safe dish and broil for 2-3 minutes until golden.*

Nutrition per Serving:
- **Calories:** 380
- **Protein:** 14g
- **Carbohydrates:** 6g
- **Fat:** 34g
- **Fiber:** 2g

2. Zucchini Noodles with Pesto Sauce

Servings: 4 • **Prep Time:** 10 minutes • **Cooking Time:** 5 minutes

Ingredients:
- 4 medium zucchinis, spiralized into noodles
- 1/2 cup fresh basil leaves
- 1/4 cup pine nuts
- 1/2 cup grated Parmesan cheese
- 2 cloves garlic, minced
- 1/2 cup olive oil
- Salt and pepper to taste

Instructions:

1.In a food processor, combine basil, pine nuts, Parmesan cheese, and garlic. Pulse until finely chopped.2. While the food processor is running, slowly drizzle in the olive oil until the pesto sauce is smooth. Season with salt and pepper.3. Heat a skillet over medium heat and sauté the zucchini noodles for 2-3 minutes until just tender.4. Toss the zucchini noodles with the pesto sauce and serve immediately.

Chef's Tip: *To avoid soggy zoodles, pat them dry with paper towels after spiralizing.*

Nutrition per Serving:
- **Calories:** 320
- **Protein:** 8g
- **Carbohydrates:** 5g
- **Fat:** 30g
- **Fiber:** 2g

3. Keto Cheesy Broccoli Casserole

Servings: 4 • **Prep Time:** 10 minutes • **Cooking Time:** 20 minutes

Ingredients:
- 4 cups broccoli florets
- 1 cup heavy cream
- 1 1/2 cups shredded cheddar cheese
- 1/2 cup cream cheese, softened
- 1/4 cup Parmesan cheese, grated
- 1/2 tsp garlic powder
- Salt and pepper to taste
- 1/4 tsp paprika (for garnish)

Instructions:

1.Preheat the oven to 375°F (190°C).2. Steam the broccoli florets for 5-7 minutes until just tender. Drain and place in a greased baking dish.3. In a saucepan, combine the heavy cream, cream cheese, cheddar cheese, garlic powder, salt, and pepper. Cook over medium heat, stirring constantly, until the cheese is melted and the sauce is smooth.4. Pour the cheese sauce over the broccoli and stir to coat evenly.5.Sprinkle the Parmesan cheese and paprika on top.6.Bake for 15-20 minutes until the top is golden and bubbly.7.Let cool slightly before serving.

Chef's Tip: *For added crunch, top the casserole with crushed pork rinds before baking.*

Nutrition per Serving:
- **Calories:** 400
- **Protein:** 15g
- **Carbohydrates:** 6g
- **Fat:** 35g
- **Fiber:** 2g

4. Roasted Brussels Sprouts with Balsamic Glaze

Servings: 4 • **Prep Time:** 5 minutes • **Cooking Time:** 25 minutes

Ingredients:
- 1 lb Brussels sprouts, trimmed and halved
- 3 tbsp olive oil
- 1/4 cup balsamic vinegar (or balsamic reduction)
- 1 tsp garlic powder
- Salt and pepper to taste
- 1 tbsp fresh parsley, chopped (for garnish)

Instructions:

1.Preheat the oven to 400°F (200°C).2.Toss the Brussels sprouts with olive oil, garlic powder, salt, and pepper.3.Spread the Brussels sprouts on a baking sheet and roast for 20-25 minutes, tossing halfway through, until golden and crispy.4.Drizzle the balsamic vinegar or reduction over the roasted Brussels sprouts and garnish with fresh parsley before serving.

Chef's Tip: *For added crunch, sprinkle the Brussels sprouts with crumbled bacon before serving.*

Nutrition per Serving:
- **Calories:** 180
- **Protein:** 4g
- **Carbohydrates:** 8g
- **Fat:** 16g
- **Fiber:** 3g

5. Keto Cauliflower Fried Rice

Servings: 4 • **Prep Time:** 10 minutes • **Cooking Time:** 10 minutes

Ingredients:

- 1 medium head cauliflower, riced (or 4 cups store-bought cauliflower rice)
- 2 tbsp coconut oil
- 2 eggs, lightly beaten
- 1/4 cup green onions, chopped
- 1/2 cup carrots, finely diced
- 2 cloves garlic, minced
- 2 tbsp soy sauce (or coconut aminos)
- 1 tsp sesame oil
- Salt and pepper to taste

Instructions:

1.Heat 1 tbsp of coconut oil in a large skillet over medium heat. Scramble the eggs and set aside.2. In the same skillet, add the remaining coconut oil and sauté the garlic, carrots, and green onions for 2-3 minutes.3. Stir in the cauliflower rice and cook for another 3-4 minutes until the cauliflower is tender.4.Add the scrambled eggs, soy sauce, sesame oil, salt, and pepper. Stir to combine and cook for an additional 1-2 minutes.5. Serve hot, garnished with extra green onions if desired.

Chef's Tip: *Add diced chicken or shrimp to make this a complete meal.*

Nutrition per Serving:

- **Calories:** 170
- **Protein:** 5g
- **Carbohydrates:** 6g
- **Fat:** 13g
- **Fiber:** 2g

6. Creamy Keto Mushroom Stroganoff

Servings: 4 • **Prep Time:** 10 minutes • **Cooking Time:** 15 minutes

Ingredients:

- 2 tbsp butter
- 1 small onion, finely chopped
- 2 cloves garlic, minced
- 10 oz mushrooms, sliced
- (cremini or white)
- 1/2 cup heavy cream
- 1/4 cup sour cream
- 1 tsp Dijon mustard
- 1/2 tsp paprika
- Salt and pepper to taste
- Fresh parsley, chopped (for garnish)

Instructions:

1.Heat butter in a large skillet over medium heat. Add the onions and garlic, sautéing for 3-4 minutes until softened.2.Add the sliced mushrooms and cook for 5-6 minutes until they release their moisture and turn golden brown.3.Stir in the heavy cream, sour cream, Dijon mustard, paprika, salt, and pepper. Simmer for 3-4 minutes until the sauce thickens.4.Garnish with fresh parsley before serving.

Chef's Tip: *Serve over zucchini noodles or cauliflower mash for a hearty meal.*

Nutrition per Serving:

- **Calories:** 280
- **Protein:** 4g
- **Carbohydrates:** 5g
- **Fat:** 26g
- **Fiber:** 1g

7. Keto Eggplant Parmesan

Servings: 4 • **Prep Time:** 10 minutes • **Cooking Time:** 25 minutes

Ingredients:

- 1 large eggplant, sliced into
- 1/2-inch rounds
- 1 cup almond flour
- 1 tsp Italian seasoning
- 1/2 tsp garlic powder
- 1 large egg, beaten
- 1 cup marinara sauce (sugar-free)
- 1 1/2 cups mozzarella cheese, shredded
- 1/2 cup Parmesan cheese, grated
- 2 tbsp olive oil
- Salt and pepper to taste

Instructions:

1.Preheat the oven to 375°F (190°C).2.In a shallow bowl, mix the almond flour, Italian seasoning, garlic powder, salt, and pepper.3.Dip each eggplant slice into the beaten egg, then coat in the almond flour mixture.4.Heat olive oil in a skillet over medium heat and fry the eggplant slices for 2-3 minutes per side until golden brown.5.Layer the fried eggplant slices in a baking dish, top with marinara sauce, mozzarella cheese, and Parmesan cheese.6.Bake for 15-20 minutes until the cheese is melted and bubbly.7.Let cool for a few minutes before serving.

Chef's Tip: *For extra flavor, sprinkle some fresh basil leaves over the top before serving.*

Nutrition per Serving:

- **Calories:** 380
- **Protein:** 15g
- **Carbohydrates:** 9g
- **Fat:** 32g
- **Fiber:** 4g

8. Cheesy Keto Cauliflower Breadsticks

Servings: 4 • **Prep Time:** 10 minutes • **Cooking Time:** 25 minutes

Ingredients:

- 1 medium head cauliflower, riced (or 4 cups store-bought cauliflower rice)
- 1 cup mozzarella cheese, shredded
- 1/2 cup Parmesan cheese, grated
- 1 large egg, beaten
- 1 tsp garlic powder
- 1 tsp Italian seasoning
- Salt and pepper to taste
- 1 tbsp fresh parsley, chopped (for garnish)

Instructions:

1.Preheat the oven to 400°F (200°C). Line a baking sheet with parchment paper.2. Steam or microwave the cauliflower rice until tender (about 5 minutes). Let cool slightly, then place the cauliflower in a clean kitchen towel and squeeze out any excess moisture.3.In a large bowl, mix the cauliflower, mozzarella cheese, Parmesan cheese, egg, garlic powder, Italian seasoning, salt, and pepper.4.Spread the cauliflower mixture onto the prepared baking sheet, forming a rectangular shape about 1/4 inch thick.5.Bake for 15-20 minutes until golden and firm.6.Remove from the oven and top with extra mozzarella cheese. Bake for an additional 5 minutes until the cheese is melted and bubbly.7. Let cool slightly before slicing into breadsticks. Garnish with fresh parsley.

Chef's Tip: *For added flavor, brush the breadsticks with melted garlic butter before serving.*

Nutrition per Serving:

- **Calories:** 250
- **Protein:** 14g
- **Carbohydrates:** 6g
- **Fat:** 19g
- **Fiber:** 2g

9. Keto Stuffed Bell Peppers with Cauliflower Rice

Servings: 4 • Prep Time: 10 minutes • Cooking Time: 30 minutes

Ingredients:

- 4 large bell peppers, tops cut off and seeds removed
- 1 lb ground beef (or turkey)
- 1 cup cauliflower rice
- 1/2 onion, diced
- 1/2 cup shredded cheddar cheese
- 1/2 cup tomato sauce (sugar-free)
- 1 tsp garlic powder
- 1 tsp Italian seasoning
- 1 tbsp olive oil
- Salt and pepper to taste

Instructions:

1.Preheat the oven to 375°F (190°C).2. In a skillet, heat olive oil over medium heat and sauté the onion for 3-4 minutes until softened. Add the ground beef and cook until browned, about 6-7 minutes. Drain excess fat.3. Stir in the cauliflower rice, tomato sauce, garlic powder, Italian seasoning, salt, and pepper. Cook for another 3-4 minutes until everything is combined and heated through.4. Stuff each bell pepper with the beef mixture and place them in a baking dish.5.Sprinkle shredded cheddar cheese on top of each stuffed pepper.6.Bake for 20-25 minutes until the peppers are tender and the cheese is melted and bubbly.7.Serve hot.

Chef's Tip: *For extra flavor, add a dash of paprika or a pinch of cayenne pepper to the egg salad mixture.*

Nutrition per Serving:

- **Calories:** 380
- **Protein:** 25g
- **Carbohydrates:** 8g
- **Fat:** 28g
- **Fiber:** 3g

10. Keto Roasted Cauliflower Steaks

Servings: 4 • Prep Time: 5 minutes • Cooking Time: 25 minutes

Ingredients:

- 1 large head of cauliflower, sliced into 1-inch thick "steaks"
- 3 tbsp olive oil
- 1 tsp garlic powder
- 1 tsp smoked paprika
- Salt and pepper to taste
- 2 tbsp fresh parsley, chopped (for garnish)

Instructions:

1.Preheat the oven to 425°F (220°C).2. Place the cauliflower steaks on a baking sheet and brush both sides with olive oil.3.Season with garlic powder, smoked paprika, salt, and pepper.4.Roast for 20-25 minutes, flipping halfway through, until the cauliflower is golden and crispy. 5.Garnish with fresh parsley before serving.

Nutrition per Serving:

- **Calories:** 160
- **Protein:** 4g
- **Carbohydrates:** 7g
- **Fat:** 14g
- **Fiber:** 3g

Chef's Tip: *For a cheesy twist, sprinkle shredded Parmesan over the cauliflower steaks during the last 5 minutes of roasting.*

CHAPTER 12
SIDES & SNACKS RECIPES

1. Keto Zucchini Fries with Garlic Aioli

Servings: 4 • **Prep Time:** 10 minutes • **Cooking Time:** 20 minutes

Ingredients:

Ingredients for Zucchini Fries:
- 2 medium zucchinis, cut into fry-like strips
- 1 cup almond flour
- 1/2 cup grated Parmesan cheese
- 1 tsp garlic powder
- 1 tsp Italian seasoning
- 2 large eggs, beaten
- Salt and pepper to taste
- Olive oil spray (for baking)

Ingredients for Garlic Aioli:
- 1/2 cup mayonnaise (keto-friendly)
- 1 clove garlic, minced
- 1 tsp lemon juice
- Salt and pepper to taste

Instructions:

1. Preheat the oven to 400°F (200°C). Line a baking sheet with parchment paper and spray with olive oil. 2. In a bowl, mix almond flour, Parmesan cheese, garlic powder, Italian seasoning, salt, and pepper. 3. Dip each zucchini strip into the beaten eggs, then coat with the almond flour mixture. 4. Place the zucchini fries on the prepared baking sheet in a single layer and spray lightly with olive oil. 5. Bake for 20 minutes, flipping halfway through, until golden and crispy. 6. While the fries bake, mix the aioli ingredients in a small bowl. 7. Serve the zucchini fries with the garlic aioli for dipping.

Chef's Tip: *For extra crispiness, broil the fries for the last 2-3 minutes.*

Nutrition per Serving:
- **Calories:** 320
- **Protein:** 12g
- **Carbohydrates:** 8g
- **Fat:** 26g
- **Fiber:** 4g

2. Keto Jalapeño Poppers with Bacon

Servings: 6 • **Prep Time:** 10 minutes • **Cooking Time:** 15 minutes

Ingredients:
- 6 large jalapeños, halved and seeded
- 4 oz cream cheese, softened
- 1/2 cup shredded cheddar cheese
- 1/4 cup shredded mozzarella cheese
- 6 slices bacon, cut in half
- 1 tsp garlic powder
- Salt and pepper to taste

Instructions:

1. Preheat the oven to 400°F (200°C). Line a baking sheet with parchment paper. 2. In a small bowl, mix the cream cheese, cheddar cheese, mozzarella cheese, garlic powder, salt, and pepper. 3. Stuff each jalapeño half with the cheese mixture. 4. Wrap each stuffed jalapeño half with a slice of bacon and place them on the prepared baking sheet. 5. Bake for 15 minutes, or until the bacon is crispy and the cheese is melted. 6. Let cool slightly before serving.

Chef's Tip: *For extra crispiness, broil the poppers for the last 2-3 minutes of baking.*

Nutrition per Serving:
- **Calories:** 220
- **Protein:** 9g
- **Carbohydrates:** 2g
- **Fat:** 20g
- **Fiber:** 1g

3. Keto Buffalo Cauliflower Bites

Servings: 4 • **Prep Time:** 10 minutes • **Cooking Time:** 25 minutes

Ingredients:

- 1 large head of cauliflower, cut into florets
- 2 tbsp olive oil
- 1/2 cup buffalo sauce (sugar-free)
- 2 tbsp butter, melted
- 1/2 tsp garlic powder
- 1/4 tsp paprika
- Salt and pepper to taste
- 1/4 cup blue cheese dressing (optional, for dipping)

Instructions:

1.Preheat the oven to 400°F (200°C). Line a baking sheet with parchment paper.2.Toss the cauliflower florets with olive oil, garlic powder, paprika, salt, and pepper.3.Spread the cauliflower on the prepared baking sheet and roast for 20 minutes, flipping halfway through.4.In a small bowl, mix the buffalo sauce and melted butter.5.Remove the cauliflower from the oven and toss it with the buffalo sauce mixture.6.Return the cauliflower to the oven and bake for an additional 5 minutes until crispy.7.Serve with blue cheese dressing, if desired.

Chef's Tip: *For extra crispiness, broil the cauliflower for the last 2 minutes.*

Nutrition per Serving:

- **Calories:** 150
- **Protein:** 2g
- **Carbohydrates:** 6g
- **Fat:** 13g
- **Fiber:** 3g

4. Parmesan-Crusted Keto Asparagus

Servings: 4 • **Prep Time:** 5 minutes • **Cooking Time:** 15 minutes

Ingredients:

- 1 bunch asparagus, trimmed
- 1/2 cup grated Parmesan cheese
- 1/4 cup almond flour
- 1 large egg, beaten
- 1/2 tsp garlic powder
- Salt and pepper to taste
- Olive oil spray (for baking)

Instructions:

1.Preheat the oven to 400°F (200°C). Line a baking sheet with parchment paper.2.In a small bowl, mix the Parmesan cheese, almond flour, garlic powder, salt, and pepper.3.Dip each asparagus spear into the beaten egg, then coat it in the Parmesan mixture.4.Place the coated asparagus spears on the baking sheet and spray lightly with olive oil.5.Bake for 12-15 minutes until golden and crispy.6.Serve hot.

Chef's Tip: *For added flavor, sprinkle the asparagus with a little lemon zest before serving.*

Nutrition per Serving:

- **Calories:** 160
- **Protein:** 7g
- **Carbohydrates:** 4g
- **Fat:** 13g
- **Fiber:** 2g

5. Keto Guacamole with Cheese Crisps

Servings: 4 • Prep Time: 10 minutes • Cooking Time: 10 min (for cheese crisps)

Ingredients:

Ingredients for Guacamole:
- 2 ripe avocados
- 1/4 cup red onion, finely diced
- 1/2 jalapeño, minced (optional)
- 1 tbsp lime juice
- 1 tbsp fresh cilantro, chopped
- Salt and pepper to taste

Ingredients for Cheese Crisps:
- 1 cup shredded cheddar cheese

Instructions:

1.Preheat the oven to 400°F (200°C). Line a baking sheet with parchment paper.2. For the cheese crisps, place small mounds (about 1 tbsp each) of shredded cheddar cheese on the prepared baking sheet, spacing them 1 inch apart.3.Bake for 8-10 minutes until the cheese is melted and crispy. Remove from the oven and let cool.4. While the crisps cool, mash the avocados in a bowl and mix in the red onion, jalapeño, lime juice, cilantro, salt, and pepper.5.Serve the guacamole with the cheese crisps for dipping.

Chef's Tip: *For a tangy twist, add diced tomatoes or a dash of cumin to the guacamole.*

Nutrition per Serving:
- **Calories:** 280
- **Protein:** 8g
- **Carbohydrates:** 6g
- **Fat:** 25g
- **Fiber:** 5g

6. Keto Spinach and Cheese Stuffed Mushrooms

Servings: 4 • Prep Time: 10 minutes • Cooking Time: 20 minutes

Ingredients:
- 12 large button mushrooms, stems removed
- 1 cup fresh spinach, chopped
- 1/2 cup cream cheese, softened
- 1/4 cup shredded mozzarella cheese
- 1/4 cup grated Parmesan cheese
- 1 clove garlic, minced
- 1 tbsp olive oil
- Salt and pepper to taste

Instructions:

1.Preheat the oven to 375°F (190°C).2.In a skillet, heat the olive oil over medium heat. Add garlic and sauté for 1 minute until fragrant.3.Add spinach and cook for 2-3 minutes until wilted. Remove from heat and mix in cream cheese, mozzarella, Parmesan, salt, and pepper.4.Stuff each mushroom cap with the spinach mixture and place them on a baking sheet.5.Bake for 15-20 minutes until the mushrooms are tender and the tops are golden.6.Let cool slightly before serving.

Chef's Tip: *For added flavor, sprinkle extra Parmesan cheese on top before baking.*

Nutrition per Serving:
- **Calories:** 220
- **Protein:** 7g
- **Carbohydrates:** 5g
- **Fat:** 18g
- **Fiber:** 1g

7. Crispy Keto Parmesan Chips

Servings: 4 • **Prep Time:** 5 minutes • **Cooking Time:** 8 minutes

Ingredients:

- 1 cup grated Parmesan cheese
- 1/2 tsp garlic powder
- 1/2 tsp Italian seasoning
- 1/4 tsp paprika (optional)

Instructions:

1.Preheat the oven to 400°F (200°C). Line a baking sheet with parchment paper.2. In a bowl, mix the Parmesan cheese, garlic powder, Italian seasoning, and paprika.3.Spoon small mounds (about 1 tablespoon) of the cheese mixture onto the baking sheet, spacing them 1 inch apart.4.Flatten the mounds slightly and bake for 5-8 minutes, or until golden and crispy. 5.Let the chips cool on the baking sheet before serving.

Chef's Tip: *For variety, try using a combination of Parmesan and cheddar cheese.*

Nutrition per Serving:

- **Calories:** 110
- **Protein:** 9g
- **Carbohydrates:** 1g
- **Fat:** 8g
- **Fiber:** 0g

8. Keto Zucchini Chips with Herb Dip

Servings: 4 • **Prep Time:** 15 minutes • **Cooking Time:** 20 minutes

Ingredients:

- 2 medium zucchinis, thinly sliced
- 2 tbsp (30ml) olive oil
- 1/2 tsp (1g) garlic powder
- 1/2 tsp (1g) onion powder
- 1/2 tsp (1g) dried oregano
- Salt and pepper, to taste

For Herb Dip:
- 1/2 cup (120g) sour cream
- 1 tbsp (15g) chopped fresh chives
- 1 tbsp (15g) chopped fresh parsley
- 1 tsp (5ml) lemon juice
- Salt and pepper, to taste

Instructions:

1.Prepare Zucchini Chips: Preheat oven to 425°F (220°C). Toss zucchini slices with olive oil, garlic powder, onion powder, oregano, salt, and pepper.2. Bake: Arrange zucchini slices in a single layer on a baking sheet. Bake for 20 minutes, or until crispy and golden, flipping halfway through. 3.Prepare Dip: In a bowl, mix sour cream, chives, parsley, lemon juice, salt, and pepper.4. Serve: Serve zucchini chips with the herb dip.

Chef's Tip: *For a savory boost, sprinkle grated Parmesan cheese on the zucchini slices before baking. The cheese will crisp up in the oven, adding extra flavor and texture to the chips.*

Nutrition per Serving:

(1/4 of chips and 1/4 of dip):

- **Calories:** 210
- **Protein:** 4g
- **Carbohydrates**: 8g
- **Fat:** 19g
- **Fiber**: 3g

9. Spicy Roasted Chickpeas Spears

Servings: 4 • **Prep Time:** 10 minutes • **Cooking Time:** 30 minutes

Ingredients:
- 1 can (15 oz or 425g) chickpeas, drained and rinsed
- 2 tbsp (30ml) olive oil
- 1 tsp (2g) smoked paprika
- 1/2 tsp (1g) cayenne pepper
- 1/2 tsp (1g) garlic powder
- 1/2 tsp (1g) onion powder
- Salt, to taste

Instructions:

1. Preheat Oven: Preheat oven to 400°F (200°C).
2. Prepare Chickpeas: Pat chickpeas dry with a paper towel.
3. Season: Toss chickpeas with olive oil, smoked paprika, cayenne pepper, garlic powder, onion powder, and salt.
4. Roast: Spread chickpeas on a baking sheet in a single layer. Roast for 30 minutes, shaking the pan halfway through, until chickpeas are crispy.

Chef's Tip: *Experiment with Seasonings: For a flavor twist, you can swap cayenne with ground cumin or add a dash of lemon zest for a citrusy zing. This can balance the spiciness and bring out new dimensions in the flavor profile.*

Nutrition per Serving:

(1/4 cup)

- **Calories:** 150
- **Protein:** 6g
- **Carbohydrates:** 13g
- **Fat:** 7g
- **Fiber**: 4g

10. Cheesy Broccoli Bites

Servings: 4(4 bites each) • **Prep Time:** 10 minutes • **Cooking Time:** 15 minutes

Ingredients:
- 2 cups (200g) broccoli florets, finely chopped
- 1 cup (100g) shredded cheddar cheese
- 1/2 cup (50g) grated Parmesan cheese
- 1/4 cup (60g) mayonnaise
- 1/2 tsp (1g) garlic powder
- 1/2 tsp (1g) dried basil
- Salt and pepper, to taste

Instructions:

1. Preheat Oven: Preheat oven to 375°F (190°C).2. Prepare Broccoli: Steam or microwave broccoli until tender. Drain and squeeze out excess moisture.3. Mix Ingredients: In a bowl, mix chopped broccoli, cheddar cheese, 4.Parmesan cheese, mayonnaise, garlic powder, dried basil, salt, and pepper.4.Form Bites: Spoon mixture into mini muffin tin cups.5.Bake: Bake for 15 minutes, or until tops are golden and cheese is melted.

Chef's Tip: *Add a Crunchy Coating: For extra texture, try sprinkling some crushed pork rinds or almond flour on top of the bites before baking. This will give them a crunchy finish without adding carbs.*

Nutrition per Serving:

(4 bites)

- **Calories**: 200
- **Protein:** 11g
- **Carbohydrates:** 8g
- **Fat:** 15g
- **Fiber**: 3g

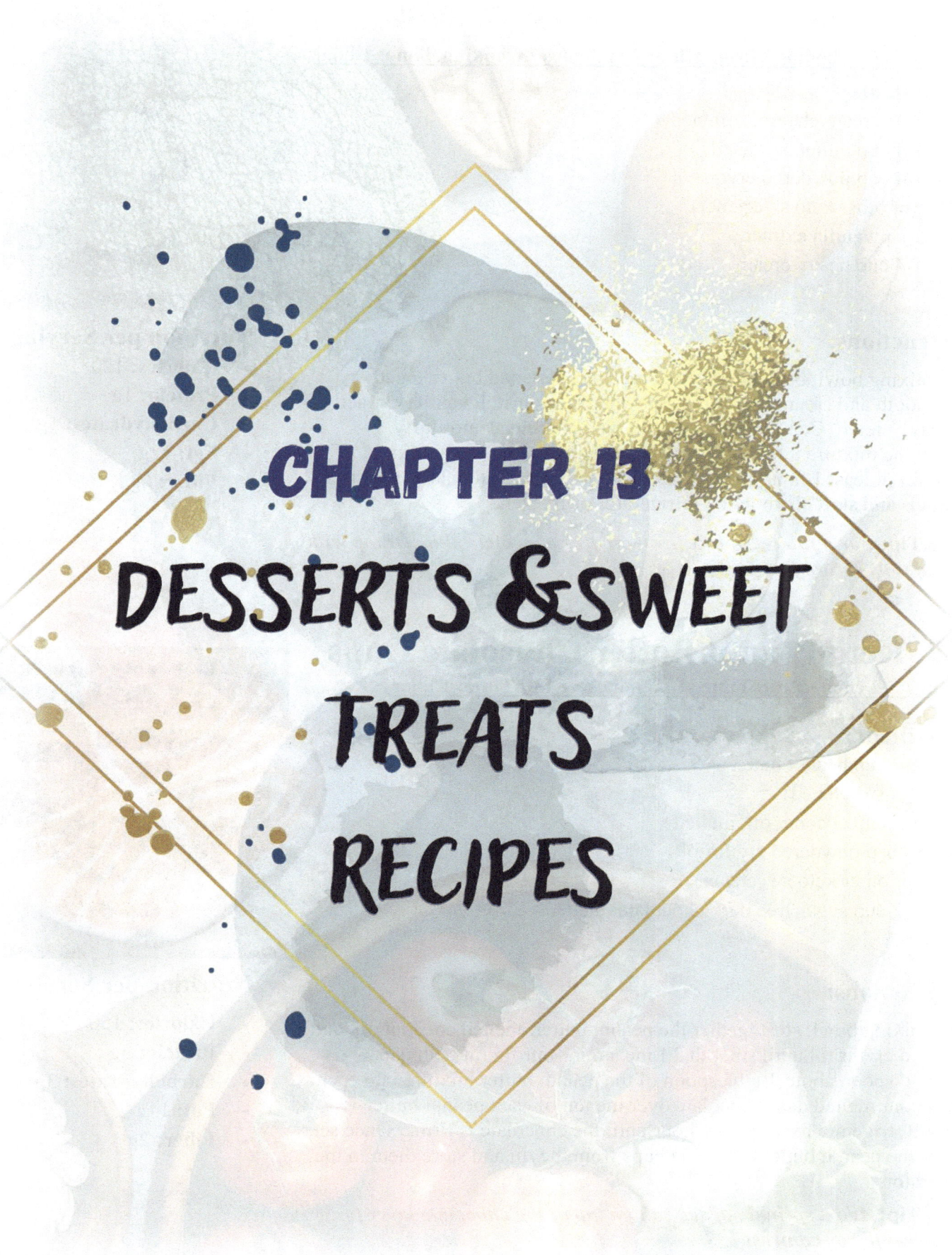

CHAPTER 13
DESSERTS & SWEET TREATS RECIPES

1. Keto Cheesecake Fat Bombs

Servings: 12 fat bombs • **Prep Time:** 10 minutes • **Cooking Time:** 1 hour

Ingredients:

- 8 oz cream cheese, softened
- 1/4 cup butter, softened
- 1/4 cup powdered erythritol
  (or other keto sweetener)
- 1 tsp vanilla extract
- 1/4 cup heavy cream

Instructions:

1.In a mixing bowl, beat the softened cream cheese and butter together until smooth and creamy.2. Add the powdered erythritol, vanilla extract, and heavy cream. Continue to beat until well combined and fluffy. 3.Scoop the mixture into silicone molds or a lined mini-muffin tin.4. Freeze for at least 1 hour until firm.5.Once set, remove the fat bombs from the molds and store them in the refrigerator or freezer.

Chef's Tip: *For a fun twist, mix in sugar-free chocolate chips or top with crushed nuts before freezing.*

Nutrition per Serving:

- **Calories:** 120
- **Protein:** 1g
- **Carbohydrates:** 1g
- **Fat:** 12g
- **Fiber:** 0g

2. Keto Peanut Butter Chocolate Cups

Servings: 12 cups • **Prep Time:** 10 minutes • **Chill Time:** 1 hour

Ingredients:

- 1/2 cup peanut butter
  (unsweetened)
- 1/4 cup coconut oil, melted
- 2 tbsp powdered erythritol
  (or other keto sweetener)
- 1/2 cup sugar-free dark chocolate, melted

Instructions:

1 In a mixing bowl, stir together the peanut butter, melted coconut oil, and powdered erythritol until smooth.2.Line a mini-muffin tin with paper liners and spoon about 1 tablespoon of the peanut butter mixture into each liner.3.Pour melted dark chocolate over the top of each peanut butter layer.4.Refrigerate for at least 1 hour until the chocolate is firm.5.Once set, remove the peanut butter chocolate cups from the tin and store them in the refrigerator.

Chef's Tip: *Add a sprinkle of sea salt on top of the chocolate layer for a salty-sweet flavor contrast.*

Nutrition per Serving:

- **Calories:** 150
- **Protein:** 3g
- **Carbohydrates:** 3g
- **Fat:** 14g
- **Fiber:** 2g

3. Keto Lemon Bars with Almond Flour

Servings: 12 bars • **Prep Time:** 10 minutes • **Cooking Time:** 30 minutes

Ingredients:

Ingredients for the Crust:

- 1 1/2 cups almond flour
- 1/4 cup powdered erythritol (or other keto sweetener)
- 1/4 cup butter, melted
- 1 tsp vanilla extract

Ingredients for the Lemon Filling:

- 3 large eggs
- 1/2 cup lemon juice (about 3 lemons)
- 1/4 cup powdered erythritol
- 1/4 cup heavy cream
- 1 tbsp lemon zest
- Pinch of salt

Instructions:

1.Preheat the oven to 350°F (175°C). Line an 8x8-inch baking dish with parchment paper.2.In a mixing bowl, combine the almond flour, powdered erythritol, melted butter, and vanilla extract. Stir until a crumbly dough forms.3.Press the dough into the prepared baking dish and bake for 10-12 minutes until golden.4.While the crust is baking, whisk together the eggs, lemon juice, powdered erythritol, heavy cream, lemon zest, and salt until smooth.5.Pour the lemon mixture over the pre-baked crust and bake for another 15-20 minutes, or until the filling is set.6.Let the lemon bars cool completely before slicing into squares

Chef's Tip: *For an extra touch, dust the top with powdered erythritol before serving.*

Nutrition per Serving:

- **Calories:** 170
- **Protein:** 4g
- **Carbohydrates:** 4g
- **Fat:** 16g
- **Fiber:** 2g

4. Keto Chocolate Chip Mug Cake

Servings: 1 • **Prep Time:** 5 minutes • **Cooking Time:** 2 minutes

Ingredients:

- 3 tbsp almond flour
- 1 tbsp coconut flour
- 1 tbsp powdered erythritol (or other keto sweetener)
- 1/2 tsp baking powder
- 1 large egg
- 1 tbsp melted butter
- 1/2 tsp vanilla extract
- 1 tbsp sugar-free chocolate chips

Instructions:

1.In a microwave-safe mug, whisk together the almond flour, coconut flour, powdered erythritol, and baking powder.2. Add the egg, melted butter, and vanilla extract. Stir until smooth.3.Fold in the sugar-free chocolate chips.4.Microwave on high for 1-2 minutes until the cake is set and puffed up.5.Let cool slightly before enjoying..

Chef's Tip: *Top with a dollop of whipped cream or a drizzle of sugar-free chocolate syrup for extra indulgence.*

Nutrition per Serving:

- **Calories:** 320
- **Protein:** 9g
- **Carbohydrates:** 6g
- **Fat:** 29g
- **Fiber:** 4g

5. Keto Coconut Macaroons

Servings: 12 macaroons • **Prep Time:** 10 minutes • **Cooking Time:** 15 min

Ingredients:

- 2 cups unsweetened shredded coconut
- 1/4 cup powdered erythritol (or other keto sweetener)
- 2 large egg whites
- 1/2 tsp vanilla extract
- Pinch of salt
- 1/4 cup sugar-free dark chocolate, melted (optional for drizzling)

Instructions:

1.Preheat the oven to 350°F (175°C) and line a baking sheet with parchment paper.2.In a bowl, whisk the egg whites with a pinch of salt until frothy.3.Fold in the shredded coconut, powdered erythritol, and vanilla extract until well combined.4.Using a spoon or cookie scoop, form small mounds of the mixture and place them on the prepared baking sheet.5.Bake for 12-15 minutes until the edges are golden brown.6.Let the macaroons cool completely. If desired, drizzle with melted sugar-free chocolate.

Chef's Tip: *For a tropical twist, mix in a tablespoon of lime zest before baking.*

Nutrition per Serving:

- **Calories:** 120
- **Protein:** 2g
- **Carbohydrates:** 4g
- **Fat:** 11g
- **Fiber:** 3g

6. Keto Pumpkin Spice Muffins

Servings: 12 muffins • **Prep Time:** 10 minutes • **Cooking Time:** 20 min

Ingredients:

- 1 1/2 cups almond flour
- 1/4 cup coconut flour
- 1/4 cup powdered erythritol
- (or other keto sweetener)
- 1 tsp baking powder
- 1 tsp pumpkin spice mix
- 1/2 cup pumpkin puree (unsweetened)
- 1/4 cup melted coconut oil
- 3 large eggs
- 1 tsp vanilla extract
- 1/4 cup unsweetened almond milk

Instructions:

1.Preheat the oven to 350°F (175°C). Line a muffin tin with paper liners. 2.In a large bowl, whisk together the almond flour, coconut flour, erythritol, baking powder, and pumpkin spice mix.3.In another bowl, mix the pumpkin puree, melted coconut oil, eggs, vanilla extract, and almond milk.4.Combine the wet and dry ingredients, stirring until just mixed. 5.Divide the batter evenly between the muffin cups and bake for 18-20 minutes, or until a toothpick inserted into the center comes out clean. 6.Let the muffins cool before serving.

Chef's Tip: *Add a handful of sugar-free chocolate chips or chopped pecans for extra flavor.*

Nutrition per Serving:

- **Calories:** 150
- **Protein:** 5g
- **Carbohydrates:** 6g
- **Fat:** 12g
- **Fiber:** 3g

7. Almond Flour Brownies

Servings: 12 brownies • **Prep Time:** 10 minutes • **Cooking Time:** 25 min

Ingredients:

- 1 1/2 cups (150 g) almond flour
- 1/2 cup (120 g) butter, melted
- 1/3 cup (50 g) unsweetened cocoa powder
- 1/2 cup (100 g) keto-friendly sweetener (e.g., erythritol)
- 3 large eggs
- 1 tsp vanilla extract
- 1/4 tsp salt
- 1/4 tsp baking powder

Instructions:

1.Preheat the oven to 350°F (175°C). Grease an 8x8-inch baking pan or line it with parchment paper.2.In a large bowl, whisk together the melted butter, eggs, and vanilla extract.3.In a separate bowl, whisk the almond flour, cocoa powder, sweetener, salt, and baking powder.4.Slowly add the dry ingredients to the wet ingredients and stir until combined.5.Pour the batter into the prepared baking pan and smooth the top.6.Bake for 20-25 minutes or until a toothpick inserted comes out clean.7.Let the brownies cool before slicing into 12 squares.

Chef's Tip: *For an extra-rich flavor, add a handful of sugar-free dark chocolate chips or chopped walnuts into the batter before baking.*

Nutrition per Serving:

(per brownie)

- **Calories**: 160
- **Protein**: 4 g
- **Carbohydrates**: 5 g
- **Fat**: 15 g
- **Fiber**: 3 g

8. Keto Strawberry Cream Popsicles

Servings: 6 popsicles • **Prep Time:** 10 minutes • **Chill Time:** 4 hours

Ingredients:

- 1 cup fresh strawberries, chopped
- 1/2 cup heavy cream
- 1/2 cup unsweetened almond milk
- 2 tbsp powdered erythritol (or other keto sweetener)
- 1 tsp vanilla extract

Instructions:

1.In a blender, combine the strawberries, heavy cream, almond milk, erythritol, and vanilla extract. Blend until smooth.
2.Pour the mixture into popsicle molds and freeze for at least 4 hours, or until solid.3.Once frozen, remove from the molds and enjoy.

Chef's Tip: *For a creamy swirl effect, reserve a few tablespoons of the blended mixture, mix with extra cream, and swirl into the popsicles before freezing.*

Nutrition per Serving:

- **Calories:** 90
- **Protein:** 1g
- **Carbohydrates:** 4g
- **Fat:** 8g
- **Fiber:** 1g

9. Sugar-Free Peanut Butter Fudge

Servings: 16 squares • **Prep Time:** 10 minutes • **Cooking Time:** 10 minutes (cooling time excluded)

Ingredients:

- 1/2 cup (125 g) natural peanut butter (unsweetened, no added sugar)
- 1/2 cup (113 g) butter
- 1/4 cup (50 g) keto-friendly sweetener (e.g., erythritol)
- 1 tsp vanilla extract
- Pinch of salt

Instructions:

1. In a small saucepan, melt the peanut butter and butter over low heat.
2. Stir in the sweetener, vanilla extract, and salt until combined.
3. Pour the mixture into a parchment-lined 8x8-inch pan and smooth the top. 4. Refrigerate for 2-3 hours or until firm. 5. Cut into 16 squares and enjoy.

Nutrition per Serving:

(per square)

- **Calories**: 120
- **Protein**: 3 g
- **Carbohydrates**: 2 g
- **Fat**: 11 g
- **Fiber**: 1 g

Chef's Tip: *For a crunchy variation, mix in a handful of chopped peanuts before pouring the fudge into the pan for added texture.*

10. Butter Pecan Fat Bombs

Servings: 12 fat bombs • **Prep Time:** 10 minutes • **Chill Time:** 1 hour

Ingredients:

- 1/2 cup (113 g) butter, softened
- 1/4 cup (56 g) cream cheese, softened
- 1/4 cup (30 g) pecans, chopped
- 2 tbsp (28 g) keto-friendly sweetener (e.g., erythritol)
- 1/2 tsp vanilla extract
- Pinch of sal

Instructions:

1. In a small skillet, toast the chopped pecans over medium heat until fragrant, about 2-3 minutes. Set aside to cool. 2. In a medium bowl, beat together the softened butter, cream cheese, sweetener, vanilla extract, and salt until smooth and creamy. 3. Fold in the toasted pecans. 4. Scoop the mixture into silicone molds or spoon onto a parchment-lined baking sheet. 5. Refrigerate for 1 hour or until firm.

Chef's Tip: *For an added crunch, mix in a tablespoon of crushed pork rinds to the fat bombs for extra texture without affecting the carbs.*

Nutrition per Serving

(per fat bomb):

- **Calories**: 120
- **Protein**: 1 g
- **Carbohydrates**: 2 g
- **Fat**: 12 g
- **Fiber**: 0.5 g

MEASUREMENT CONVERSION TABLES

VOLUME EQUIVALEN TS (LIQUID)

US STANDART	US STANDART (OUNCES)	METRIC (APPROXIMATE)
2 tablespoons	1 fl.oz.	30 ml
¼ cup	2 fl.oz.	60 ml
½ cup	4 fl.oz.	120 ml
1 cup	8 fl.oz.	240 ml
1½ cup	12 fl.oz.	355 ml
2 cups or 1 pint	16 fl.oz.	475 ml
4 cups or 1 quart	32 fl.oz.	1 L
1 gallon	128 fl.oz.	4 L

OVEN TEMPERATURES

FAHRENHEIT (F)	CELSIUS (C) (APPROXIMATE)
250°F	120°C
300°F	150°C
325°F	165°C
350°F	180°C
375°F	190°C
400°F	200°C
425°F	220°C
450°F	230°C

VOLUME EQUIVALENTS (DRY)

US STANDART	US STANDART (OUNCES)
¼ teaspoon	1 ml
½ teaspoon	2 ml
1 teaspoon	5 ml
1 tablespoon	15 ml
¼ cup	59 ml
⅓ cup	79 ml
½ cup	118 ml
1 cup	235 ml

WEIGHT EQUIVALENTS

US STANDART	METRIC (APPROXIMATE)
½ ounce	15g
1 ounce	30g
2 ounces	60g
4 ounces	115g
8 ounces	225g
12 ounces	340g

FAQs with straightforward answers to help beginners

Starting a ketogenic diet can raise a lot of questions, especially for those new to the concept of carbohydrate restriction and ketosis. Here are some of keto newbies' most frequently asked questions, answered in clear and understandable terms to ease the transition and improve your understanding of this dietary approach.

→ *What Foods Can I Eat on a Keto Diet?*

Fatty meats, fish, butter and cream, cheese, nuts and seeds, avocados, and low-carb vegetables such as leafy greens are foods to focus on in a keto diet. Prioritizing foods rich in healthy fats and proteins while keeping your carbohydrate intake low is essential.

→ *What Should I Avoid Eating on a Keto Diet?*

You should avoid sugar, grains and starches, high-carb fruits, and legumes on a keto diet. You should also limit root vegetables like potatoes and carrots and sugary snacks and desserts.

→ *How Many Carbs Can I Eat on a Keto Diet?*

Typically, the keto diet restricts your carb intake to about 20 to 50 grams per day. This varies based on individual metabolism and exercise levels. Tracking your carbs can help you stay within this range to maintain ketosis.

→ *What are the Benefits of a Keto Diet?*

The keto diet can lead to significant weight loss and improvements in blood sugar control, which can be particularly beneficial for those with type 2 diabetes. Many also report enhanced mental focus and sustained energy levels throughout the day.

→ *Are There Any Side Effects?*

Some people may experience the "keto flu," including symptoms like headache, fatigue, and irritability as their bodies adjust. These symptoms typically resolve after a few days to weeks as their bodies adapt to burning fat for fuel.

→ *Can I Drink Alcohol on a Keto Diet?*

Yes, but choose wisely. Opt for low-carb options like spirits or dry wines, and avoid sugary cocktails and beers.

→ *What is a Typical Day on a Keto Diet Like?*

A typical day might include a breakfast of eggs and bacon, a lunch of avocado salad with grilled chicken, and a dinner of salmon with asparagus. Snacks could include cheese, nuts, or olives.

→ *How Do I know if I'm in Ketosis?*

Common indicators include increased urination, dry mouth, bad breath, and reduced hunger. You can also use ketone urine testing strips to check your ketone levels.

→ *Can I Still Eat Out While on the Keto Diet?*

Yes, focus on meals cantered on proteins and vegetables, and be mindful of hidden sugars and carbs in sauces and dressings.

→ *How Fast Will I Lose Weight?*

Weight loss can vary, but many people see rapid weight loss initially due to reduced carb intake and water loss. After this initial phase, weight loss may stabilize.

→ *Is the Keto Diet Safe Long-Term?*

While many people thrive on a keto diet long-term, focusing on nutrient-rich foods is essential to ensure a balanced intake. Consulting with healthcare providers is recommended.

→ *Do I Need to Count Calories?*

Not necessarily, but it is crucial to be mindful of portion sizes and the types of food consumed. The focus should be on the quality of the diet.

→ *How Can I Avoid Common Mistakes on the Keto Diet?*

Common mistakes include not eating enough fat, consuming too much protein, and neglecting to drink enough water. Staying informed and mindful can help avoid these pitfalls.

Thank you so much for purchasing The Keto Diet Cookbook for Beginners! I hope these recipes inspire and guide you to healthier eating, making keto delicious and easy to follow♥️

For the United States

For the United Kingdom

Dear readers, I have put all my heart and love into creating this book to help you on your keto diet journey. Each dish is made with your health and taste preferences in mind, and I sincerely hope they will become your favorites every day. If you liked the recipes, please share your opinion by leaving a **review on Amazon via the QR code** that you will find in the book.

Your feedback inspires me to create new recipes and cookbooks, and I can't wait to find out which dishes brought you joy. Thank you for choosing my book for your culinary journey!

🎁 **Dear readers, remember to pick up three special bonuses** 🎁 :

"10 Keto Asian Recipes"
"10 Keto Italian Recipes"
"10 Keto Mexican Recipes"
These additional recipes will help you diversify your keto menu and make the holidays even more delicious. May every day in the kitchen bring you joy and new culinary discoveries!

Made in the USA
Las Vegas, NV
16 February 2025

18209299R00044